The Existence Paradox
and the Ineffable Nature of Reality

by

Christian Reinhardt

Vedanta Publishing
Edmonton, Canada

The Existence Paradox and the Ineffable Nature of Reality
Copyright © 2024, Christian Reinhardt

ISBN: 978-1-7780839-1-4

First German print edition, 2004

First English print edition, March 2024

Published by Vedanta Publishing

This book is dedicated to
Benjamin Creme

Cover image: The cover design depicts the hand-brushed circular shape known in Zen Buddhism as an *Ensō* (representing Śūnyatā or emptiness) encircling and containing within it the Earth (depicting the form world). The *Ensō* is a sacred symbol representing the interconnectedness of all things, the timeless Now, and the formless Nondual 'nature' of Cosmos from which the form world arises to demonstrate the illusion of duality and multiplicity.

Table of Contents

Wittgenstein: "Whereof one cannot speak,
one has to be silent about"

Reinhardt: "Whereof one cannot speak,
one has to write about"

Foreword

When I'm asked what my book is about, I'm always extremely reluctant to say 'philosophy', even less so to say 'religion', usually ending up with 'insight' and not feeling any better. Maybe I am just too shy to say 'wisdom'.

The subsequent question is often then, "Is it complicated?" Philosophy is generally considered complicated. Some passages in the book are actually quite specific. It was my thesis at the Faculty of Philosophy, in sinology to be precise, and yet I wrote for everyone and tried to be as comprehensible as possible.

Philosophy literally means "love of wisdom," which is really what it's all about. Probably Spirituality is the best word for what is so difficult to label. In the last instance, it is about the synthesis of spirituality and politics.

The 'magic word' of Chinese thinking appears both in the old transcription Tao and in the new better one: Dao.

The 'magic word' of Buddhist thought appears throughout in the transcription Sunyata – one pronounces it "shoon-YAH-tah." It is a word from the ancient Indian scholarly language Sanskrit. In English, it is translated as *Emptiness*. Chinese would say *Kong* (pronounced 'koong").

The most characteristic word about philosophy was probably T.W. Adornos' "Philosophy is the most serious thing in the world, but not that serious" ("Die Philosophie ist die ernsteste Sache der Welt, aber so ernst auch wieder nicht"). This book contains explanations about a historical process, the so-called "end of philosophy" announced for over a hundred years. It is also the product of a successful balancing act in the art of living. It is the document of the

1

compromise of my life: in the so-called humanities there is no such thing as something that could possibly correspond to what in the natural sciences is so neatly called the current state of research. For someone who is serious about the question of what Spirit (Geist) might mean, contemporary humanities at the university level is not a particularly suitable platform for practicing the art of Self-realization, which is what matters, after all, given that human existence seeks meaning. Nevertheless, this has been my pursuit.

My favorite theologian, Romano Guardini (1885-1968), taught at the same university where I was privileged to study and left the following words that could also speak for me: "It's reassuring, that the university recognizes you. It is somehow my unhappy love, i.e. it's not quite true like that, it's more complicated. I love the university, every time I come near her I'm happy. And yet I keep getting the feeling that I actually have no right to be in it. The standard that applies in it and after you belong to it is science, but I am not a scientist. The self-evidence of belonging was missing: basically, I never asked what my listeners wanted to know, but talked about what was important to myself. I had the perhaps presumptuous but vivid certainty that the things that interested me were worth saying. It was so that quite a number of my books said their things, as it were, one hour earlier than the general public became aware of wanting to hear anything about them. I have never written a book because I thought the time or a purpose demanded it but always only because I was prompted to do so from the inside."

The compromise I made with Ludwig Maximilian University Munich, despite many internal academic limitations it imposed on me, was a fruitful one.

The author comes from a country known as the land of poets and thinkers: Germany. Three of the four main figures in this manuscript are German-language authors: Heidegger,

Wittgenstein and Jean Gebser (1905-1973). The fourth main figure is Indian, by name Nagarjuna (circa. 150-250 AD). Heidegger, Wittgenstein and Gebser have been translated into English differently at times before. In many places, I have attempted to offer my own German to English translation; in other places I have tried to find the most commonly agreed upon translation. In some rare cases, I have left the original German expression in place for the reader to work with on their own. I have left in the source citations as the original German-language book title for those who would like to retrace my steps.

Finally, due to the variety of sources which I have drawn upon for my research, the reader may encounter both the new and old form of Chinese transcription.

My thanks, above all, go to Todd Lorentz for publishing my book. I'm not sure whether I would want to know how many free hours he offered up in correcting my translation, which I did originally with the help of translation software. I simply couldn't accept such love, support, diligence and care except that I know it is an expression of a global co-operation, of which we both are happy to be a part. It is a work initiated by Benjamin Creme (1922-2016) to whom we owe the suggestion for the English version of this book. I would also like to thank Eric Sachs for his assistance and skill in translating some of the most difficult German expressions into English, and to Ray Shaw and Jessie Webster for their assistance in developing the cover and support with the eBook formatting.

Christian Reinhardt
Munich, 2024

Preface

But with the end of philosophy the thinking is not at the end, but in the transition to another beginning.[1]

Martin Heidegger

The truth was once sought: For thousands of years philosophy has done this work. The truth was once believed: For thousands of years the "relegio" and later religion made this binding possible. Always also, where we think or believe, what is attainable with it will be unloseable. For those, however, who are able to preserve the whole, the true, this true is no longer a philosophical search, nor a faith that can always also be in doubt, but a finding without that search, which through millennia was, as it were, only preparation.[2]

Jean Gebser

"Does philosophy still have meaning and value?" asks Hans-Joachim Störig as a conclusion to the new edition of his *Little World History of Philosophy*. He continues: "Such questions must also be asked because, after all, leading, 'ordered' professional representatives of philosophy – think of Heidegger and Wittgenstein – themselves undertake, demand or promise a 'destruction' and an end, a definitive completion of all earlier philosophies!"

Starting from this question, I, Christian Reinhardt, born 74 years after the two above-mentioned ordered representa-

---

[1] Heidegger, Martin: *Vorträge und Aufsätze*, Pfullingen, 1990, p.79.

[2] Gebser, Jean: *Gesamtausgabe Band 3*, Schaffhausen, 1978, p.689.

4

tives of philosophy, develop my thoughts – referring back to the two again and again.

Where do we stand today in light of this inventory? What is philosophy in the face of its end? Many other voices are heard including two thinkers who were bold enough to suggest how to baptize what may come after the destruction of philosophy.

It was then about this study of which the two 'bold proposers' had inspired me with their writings that I embarked upon my final thesis for the M.A. degree *Chinese Buddhist Thought and Western Philosophy: An Assessment in the subject Sinology*. But it is not so much a 'scientific treatise', even if the rhythm of life wanted me to present it as one in order to be recognized as such. To what extent my text corresponds to a different calling might be called into question. The first and actual style of my efforts is an "enlightening-explanatory" one, which sometimes includes a "philosophy-story-telling" one.

Even the writing of a philosophical book is questionable for the "spark" ignites only in genuine dialogue. Plato, for whom it is said that the whole of Western philosophy is a footnote, is supposed to have said "there is no writing of mine, and there never will be; for it cannot be uttered like something that can be learned, but it…suddenly arises, as if ignited by a leaping spark, a light in the Soul emerges, which from now on sustains itself."

So the philosophers after Plato left us their monologues, which is alright. The only all-too-human mistake was that the whole thing, even today, slips again and again into the unreal discussion of "which monologue is the right monologue." The previous philosophers also had the desire to match their monologues with reality. Here it is so important to recall what Heidegger admitted in his letter to Hartmut Buchner (1927-2004), who was my Heidegger teacher at LMU (University Munich) – he has "no evi-

5

dence" that what he said "is consistent with reality," above all, "never binding as a statement."[3]

Also Wittgenstein's most important contribution was to insist that a word *cannot* coincide with reality at all. A large part of the beginning of my work is devoted to the elucidation of this claim. Nevertheless, I want to explain it here again from another point of view, because it seems to me to be the decisive one.

One fundamental aspect of all distinctions, which I personally learned and internalized through the continuous repetition in Hellmut Wolff's (1906-1986) lectures – between knowledge on the one hand and insight on the other hand – already exists in Plato (Doxa vs. Episteme) but is unfortunately mostly ignored at the university. This often culminates in the belief that the knowledge of a philosophical *wording* is all there is to find out. But the question is: When is the knowledge of a philosophical wording or concept *connected* with an insight? When is it really a discovery or 'revelation' in contrast to mere factual knowledge? The discovery or revelation is not in the wording, but in the vibration or the content that the wording is supposed to convey. This is what makes philosophy so difficult. I might put it as follows: what makes the insight the *insight* is not the mere verbalization of the insight. It may be that sometimes it works, and a description hits a certain resonance in someone's consciousness which then signifies the findings, but this does not happen automatically with the description. This is precisely, as I see it, the basic reality, and the basic dilemma of all human philosophical endeavors. The fact that this basic reality is almost never recognized, let alone

---

[3] Heidegger, Martin; *Vorträge und Aufsätze*, Pfullingen, 1990, p.177-179. "keine Ausweiskarte," dass das von ihm "Gesagte mit der Wirklichkeit übereinstimmend" sei, vor allem "nie verbindlich als Aussage."

taken into account, is probably due to the fact that it was not seen clearly enough by previous philosophers and, thus, was not singled out as a basic reality. So to put it slightly differently, *experience and verbalization of experience will always remain two separate domains!* The richness of the history of philosophy will not be fully appreciated until the conditions that have made philosophy impossible have been made transparent – the previous philosophies from throughout world history were 'only' verbalizations and were aware of this only limitedly.

To become fully aware of it could be paraphrased as follows: *In the exact moment of the naming of a (philosophical) sentence, the same thing will not necessarily play out in the consciousness of one listener and in the consciousness of another listener. To recognize this fact, to see this dilemma would not only mean to accept the non-communicability of philosophy, it's not-in-itself existence independent of an interpreting brain, but also to stop misusing (philosophical) language.*

But the relation between experience and verbalization has another dimension which turns everything upside down. When I said earlier "what makes the insight the insight is not the mere verbalization of the insight" I must add that, on the other hand, there also can be no insight without verbalization. An insight cannot exist if it is not verbalized.

Let me give you a stark example. On the occasion of the birth of her granddaughter, my godmother wrote me a very cordial letter among other things with the question "Where is your soul found?" I wrote to her, but I could hardly answer her to the best of my ability despite the most intensive reading of the "ageless wisdom" (*philosophia perennis*). It would be easier for those who do not believe in an existence of something like "soul." My distinction is always that between soul and psyche. Simplified I would say, the psyche is the place of emotions and also thoughts, while the soul is that which is postulated since primeval memory by the philosophers and the religious thinkers and poets. It can be described in my experience, most likely, as a place of wordless transcendence. Even with an acceptance of such a "definition" the problem would remain that for us language-beings nothing can be real which we do not baptize. So only by naming things do they become what they are. "No thing where the word is missing," so says Heidegger. The experience of "wordless transcendence" would be bound to the verbalization of "wordless transcendence," which is a contradiction in itself. Here I have to "give in a little." Except for a few representatives of contemporary philosophy who recognize the "contradiction in itself," the paradox is a fruitful main theme of true thinking. It is only in these recent times that I have first heard a lecture from a living philosopher, until now unknown to me, who presents on "The common form of distinctions, signs and paradoxes."

This is, in my opinion, one of the primordial paradoxes of life: it exists independently of whether we verbalize, but only when we verbalize does it become real for us in the sense of "conceiving" (hence, "concept"). On the one hand, experience is always pre-verbal. On the other hand, "things are what the word makes of them by naming them."

Both basic realities are true. Reality and language are always separate realms. And the opposite is also true. Only language makes reality.

My soul is in the place of 'languagelessness', I am tempted to say.

That thinker of the 20th century whom I consider to be *the* pioneering one (because of the context he has set up with his work) has written in detail about what he sees is the fundamental difference in the endings "-less" or "-free." Thus he makes the difference between timelessness and time-free-ness – which to explain would be to outline his work, which I cannot do here. His name is Jean Gebser. So I have to correct myself, and it really makes a difference. My soul finds itself at the place of language-free-ness – which is free to bring forth a word, or even 'only' intonate a word inside, *soundlessly*.

Matthias Varga von Kibéd has given a good proposal for defining 'paradox': "A paradox is not an object, but the description of a transitional state in a process." So life is a paradox, which permanently changes over in the transition from language-free-ness to language. Except that language-free-ness and language are opposites – and there you are, what they actually are not. As I have tried to explain, the fact that they are opposites from a certain point of view but not opposites at all is really not easy to understand. A template that has served me well is what in Buddhism is called "the two truths." The crystallization of the "two truths" as the deep structure of Buddhism forms a part of the inner framework of this book.

You could call the structure of this book cumulative. It does indeed have a pre-announced peak towards the end. In reality, this is to be looked at differently. The climax in itself, properly understood, is not a point and does not come at the end but is permanent. But this is also not quite correct. The problem is the category "is." And it is precisely this that the climax lacks. It has no "is." It is not a "something" at all. So, nothing? Yes, similar to nothing and yet different. I have set out to explain the latter to the best of my ability. In a combination of tradition-steadiness alongside my own ways of thinking I have tried to show what "I may perceive whatever holds the world together in its inmost folds." (Goethe) – why we will never understand it and nevertheless can think of it as intuition, although it has no "is."

The early Heidegger uses the spelling "Seyn" which was transferred to English as Beyng. But he has invented another stylistic device to illustrate his insight. It is supposed to express the missing "is" of Being. I have re-explained this stylistic device, used it further and – with respect – improved it. Yes, I must say corrected it.

In the note on the basic questions formulated by Heidegger as "hints," he writes:

Carry in front of you, the one "who": Who is man?	Trag vor dir her das eine wer: wer ist der Mensch?
Say one thing without ceasing: What is Beyng?	Sag ohne Unterlass das eine was: was ist das Seyn?

He further writes:

> The notion of Beyng has overcome the end of "philosophy." However, opposition to "philosophers" does not throw it out of friendship with the thinkers.[4]

With the almost simultaneous appearance of Freud, Reich, Jung, Adler, Rank, Asssagioli, Gurdijeff, etc., the former of the two basic questions received a groundbreaking impetus. Thus, the interface of philosophy and psychology is also a recurring motif of this book. A later generation of psychologists was to introduce a term that I think is very useful. It is the "inner child." The author is true to the experience of the inner child as himself. For me, this book is nothing less (or nothing more) than the triumph of the inner child. Anyone who gets through this book to the end will know what I mean.

In the last days of writing my final thesis for an M.A. degree, my state of mind was strongly influenced by the

---

[4] Heidegger, Martin. *Aus der Erfahrung des Denkens*, Frankf./M., 1983, p.33.

power of Jiddu Krishnamurti. I devoured the biography just published by Vanamali Gunturu, whom I had met earlier while studying. Deeply familiar with Krishnamurti's lectures via video and literature for years, this refresher inspired me with the courage to bring up the last sequences fragmentarily, sometimes unrelated.

At one point the dissolution of philosophy in the 20th century is put into relation with the dissolution of the classical music structure in the same period. Mathias Spahlinger has the floor. Of the countless composers I have heard he is the one who most clearly crystallizes the theory of New Music as distinct from classical music. The comparison of New Music and the replacement of philosophy will be a landmark when later generations look back on our time. That New Music was faster in its development than the replacement of philosophy is bluntly shown by the fact that the name "New Music" existed right after the beginning of the 20th century, while the discipline that replaced (or is to replace) philosophy still has no generally accepted name!

At the time of writing this work I assumed that, in addition to the two namings I was aware of for the new field, there would be other proposals from more recent thinkers. Today I doubt that there are so many proposals. Whether or not the synopsis put forward by Jean Gebser on his interpretation of history is accepted, the power and overarching distinctions of his proposal will inevitably prevail in the long run due to its foundational permeability. Probably one of the most momentous quotations of this book, which you hold in your hands, reads:

> This should be noted: the systematic philosophy of individual influence is over. [...] Eteology takes the place of

philosophy, just as philosophy once took the place of myths.[5]

The specification that Gebser gives following this quotation will have to be cracked.[6] Of course, this can only be done if an effort is made to include at least the context he outlines in his writings in the discussion. His terminology about human evolution is reproduced in my work. The first biography about him I received, unfortunately, only after completion of my work was already submitted. There, in a diary note he names today's present state as an alternative formulation to the one he chose for his work: "We are without doubt, in these immediate years, in the transition from one sharply defined part of the great Platonic solar year to the next."[7]

That I once had a hypothetical eteologist whisper that an individual cannot acquire the title of eteologist, seems to me established in the above quotation. Nevertheless, accordingly in the style of Heidegger:

> The notion of Beyng is explained anew and with it the end of philosophy is actually complete. Behind the scenery eteology is waiting to be revealed. However, the opposition to intellectualism (academism) does not throw

---

[5] Gebser, Jean; *Ursprung und Gegenwart*, 2.Teil (Gesamtausgabe Band 3, Schaffhausen, 1978, p.418).

[6] An important distinction must be made here with regard to the word "eteology", which should not be confused with the common term "etiology." Gebser, in essence, invented the word "eteology" as derived from the Greek word *eteos*, an adjective meaning *true* or *genuine*. Eteology, then, is the Study of the True or Genuine.

[7] Wehr, Gerhard; Jean Gebser, *Individuelle Transformation vor dem Horizont eines neuen Bewusstseins*, Petersberg, 1996, p.129.

12

eteology out of friendship with the real insight which underlies some intellectualism.

No one should be put off by what may sound "technical" or "jargon(y)" in the chapter headings. The outer framework of this book came into being, as I said, because the rhythm of life still vibrates in the old beat (belief in titles, authorities, etc., which basically means a subtle form of commercialization, money worship, the only 'true' religion of mankind). I wrote my master's thesis not only for my professor and me, but for everyone. To ensure the enjoyment of some 'delicacies' within this book for the reader it is necessary to make a small guarantee: the pages of this book are actually the original text as I submitted it.

A piece by the Russian composer Sophia Gubaidulina, who lives near Hamburg, has the lines:

When is it really over?
What's a boundary?
Tomorrow we'll play a different game.

What considerations came about during the writing of this thesis is hinted at in a portion from a letter I wrote to Pivi (Dr. Phil. Lisa Kock, my godmother):

The truth is drastic: not only do we fail to discover our potential, let alone draw it out, but we push it back through our state education. The university, like the school, is a system that prevents creativity, but doesn't even realize that it prevents creativity, and thus doesn't even raise the real question of how it prevents creativity. I am convinced that creativity is far more than we know so far. I know one in whose speaking the word creativity is so clothed that what I feel is the promise of that word comes across. It is the Indian Jiddu Krishnamurti. Just this much: Krishnamurti's concept of creativity resonates far above the usual connotations of creativity.

13

In a letter to a religious philosopher I saw on television (Robert Spaemann), and who I had asked to send me the wording of one of his sentences uttered there (because I felt in this sentence the link between wisdom and beauty that appeals to me more than anything else), I introduced myself through the following statement:

> Unfortunately, in my master's work, the beauty aspect had to take a back seat somewhat to a more important one, which in all humility I can only call "Spiritual indignation."
>
> Among other things, I think it is didactically irresponsible not to take seriously the more than hundred year old keyword of the "overcoming of philosophy" (Nietzsche, Heidegger, Wittgenstein, also Sartre, Derrida, etc.). I believe that the history of philosophy from Plato to Wittgenstein marks an age which is now coming to an end. In my experience, no one has laid this out as clearly as Jean Gebser. It is around him that I have built my work.

The mental indignation experienced its pacification in the triumph of the inner child. The inner child says "I have no sense at all to understand why what I have to say should be evaluated. I don't even understand what evaluation is supposed to be." The adult, who remembers his dignity as the "inner child," says "I will not be evaluated."

Under the general structure "philosophy is education," which takes up the preface, it is certainly the most courageous contribution of the inner child to reject a classification in the number system of one to six. I knew that the undertaking would go well because my main professor could not doubt the genuineness of my modest appearance in the university.

I received further confirmation when I read in the magazine *Share International (April 2000)* a book review under the title "Debating the real issues of education" written by Alfie Kohn and titled *The schools our children deserve: Moving beyond traditional classrooms and "tougher standards"* (Houghton Mifflin, Boston, 1999):

> Kohn cites findings from numerous studies and concludes that grades and test scores – the main concern of the 'Old School' actually hinder children's natural curiosity and need to learn. The matter of grading, and the effect on students' motivation, becomes even worse when grades are used to rank students, causing them to dislike school and prefer, where possible, less challenging tasks to secure the highest possible grade for the least amount of work, with hardly any or no learning taking place. **"If competition," says Kohn, "were a consumer product rather than an ideology, it would have been banned long ago."** (emphasis mine)

At last I read from another mouth the consequence that had long been clear to me – especially as far as the humanities faculties of the university were concerned:

> ...the questions students ask must be the guidelines for the curriculum.

and,

> Kohn's objections are not limited to the American school system. He subverts traditional views of teaching and learning with a comprehensive and insightful vision of education and inspires hope for the future of schools and, by extension, society worldwide.

My book is also dedicated to this hope which is the only realistic hope we have.

Kohn's key phrase, "Desire to learn must not be stimulated, but kept from going out." This is even better because it is a more stark formulation than that made by Ron Smothermon alongside my own opening statements, which all act as the prelude to this book – *The Existence Paradox*. The *artifice* of this work is that I had to sell it as a "scientific work" – and yet it obeys a different principle, always trying to present that as well.

During my studies (sinology, philosophy, religious studies), I noticed what a strange agreement there was between many a lecturer and some students at times when the word "scientific relevance" abruptly broke into the conversation, as if there were "scientific" sentences and "less scientific" sentences in this disciplinary field – and the scientific ones were then the valuable ones and the less scientific ones not so valuable (as if a *sentence* in this disciplinary field could have scientific relevance or not). This strange agreement is a stubborn symptom of the takeover by the natural sciences which shape current interpretations of the world. In truth, it is a not really an intelligent form of what might best be described as the attachment to a disavowed world skepticism and its pseudo-ironic code – "being critical" – which then finds its illusory fulcrum in the irrational idolatry of an unquestioned word called "scientificity." This results from, to put it succinctly, a lack of feeling for "vibration" – that is, a sense for deep truths, which are present in ancient wisdom texts.

What is or is not titled "scientific" in humanities university seminars is probably one of the most pernicious of all non-distinguishing *distinctions*, which is (admittedly, slightly) partly responsible for steering the human potential of young people in the wrong directions, or holding it back altogether.

As a concession to the opponents of the potentially explorable sounding word '*Spirituality*', I could make the statement "Spirituality is just 'consolation'" – 'consolation' with the respect to the fact that perhaps the greatest thing a human being can achieve, depending on which connotation of 'consolation' he allows, my book barely offers. From a paper I wrote on Ignatius, "Consolation for Ignatius is being always open to the gracious immediacy of the influx and touch of divine loving kindness."

From one of my favorite books *Weltrevolution der Seele* (World Revolution of the Soul, Zürich, 1993 by Sloterdijk/Macho) I offer the following words of Adorno:

> Philosophy, as it can only be justified in the face of despair, would be the attempt to look at all things as they appear from the point of view of salvation.

That part of my consciousness – however small it may be (that is redeemed) – therefore needs no consolation to call it awareness and it is from that source which has written this Master's thesis.

Here's what really happened. An assertion by Arnold Keyserling about the Chinese language, in the context of the dawn of the New Age, led me into Sinology. I studied Sinology not out of any particular interest in China but because it was on my path of knowledge regarding the question of what may be behind the 'overcoming of philosophy'. So it's not really technical literature.

I have written with a view to publication for a more general audience, setting down my path of knowledge along with the contribution of sinology. The headings, of course, had to sound 'sinological'. Even the original title *Chinese, Buddhist Thought and Western Philosophy: An appreciation* was in some ways just like a cover. It is basically about providing the public with a document with the balancing act in the successful art of living. My book could be called a wolf in sheep's clothing, when in fact it is actually a sheep in wolf's clothing.

Unfortunately, I got hold of the first Jean Gebser biography only after I had finished my work. Otherwise I could have added the following excerpt by the Indologist Georg Feuerstein:

> Gebser's outstanding achievement is to have specified the determinants of the individual types of consciousness and thus to have created completely new possibilities of knowledge. Besides their importance for psychology, anthropology, mythology, symbolism, and philosophy, his proofs are also of special significance for all those fields of knowledge which deal with non-Western cultural goods, such as Indology, Sinology, or African studies.

It may be that Gebser had a controversial personality, but the academic world's previous ignorance of Gebser is just one of several examples showing that an 'uncompromising love of wisdom' within universities has, for some time now, only existed in exceptional cases.

Introduction

Culture confronts each one of us with a single task: to foster the generation of the philosopher, the artist, and the saint within us and outside us, and thereby to work towards the perfection of nature.[8]

$\updownarrow$

Our culture does not encourage people to be philosophers, and this is perhaps the most devastating denial of freedom in our lives.[9]

Philosophy is the poorest and highest of the arts. It cannot be taught and, in some respects, cannot be lived because it is not noticeable. Yes, it cannot even be depicted (represented), as I will show in this work.

I write a sentence and realize how relative it is. It is merely one of many points of view. What I wrote could have been seen, reformulated, from another completely different point of view. Philosophy is impossible. Or else it would have to integrate all perspectives side by side.

As one of the most important principles of Western philosophy – "I know that I do not know" – remains valid also for this master's thesis. So I don't want to write an "I know what" work, which would really only be an "I forgot that I

---

[8] Nietzsche, Friedrich; *Gesamtausgabe* Vol.III/1: Geburt der Tragödie. Unzeitgemäße Betrachtungen, Berlin, N.Y., 1984, p.378.

[9] Bartley,W.W., *Biography of Werner Erhard, the Transformation of a man*, N.Y., 1978, p.184.

don't know" work. Most likely it would be an "In the following lies clarity for me" work, or a "thoughts to be described have developed scope in my mind" work. A problem, however, is that the clarity or the scope to use this term, which is decisive for the evaluation of philosophy,[10] has developed over a longer period of time from about fifteen years – from my age 18 until 33 (1981-1996).

Now some things are presented here which have just been thought out, or thought about in a process, and then it sounds as if once again someone is speaking who thinks that he knows. So let me first repeat: I know that I do not know. And even more clearly (a bit self-mocking): I know that I have nothing to say, and do not belong to those who have nothing to say but do not know that they have nothing to say.

We live in a time without philosophical culture, i.e. life is not experienced in a way in which it would be interpreted as most adequately as possible as a kind of species-wide "insight gathering process" or something more simplistically formulated – insight accumulation. Since we are not philosophically up to date (that is, within the state of things philosophically speaking) – in order to show that this must necessarily be a high motivation for this work – it follows that certain basic requirements of a conventional work on philosophy and the basic premises of a master's thesis are actually no longer very suitable to present the notions or ideas for what, by any other name at present, might be called "transformation." We live in a time of upheaval.

---

[10] The other yardstick for philosophy is exhilaration (cf. Nietzsche: "The true thinker always refreshes, whether he expresses his seriousness or his jest, his human insight or his divine forbearance," from Gamm, *Nietzsches Botschaft f. d. Gegenwart*, München, 1993, p.297).

Much will depend on man's ability to renounce outworn structures.[11]

When the old structures no longer work, but new ones are not yet in place, this results in a variety of transitional situations. One such situation is the assignment of a master's thesis in the style of the old age, interestingly enough focused exclusively on one of three subjects the student had to take.

It is essential to state some basic facts about learning. Anyone who has observed a baby or a child with alert eyes and intelligence knows that playing is the archetype or original form of learning or, more precisely, learning is the archetype of playing(!). If learning is no longer fun, something has gone wrong – the experiment on self-education of the humans went wrong and so the experiment of mankind has so far gone wrong.

> Children have a natural desire to know, to learn and to participate. We send our kids to school where they are treated *as if they did not want to learn* and we treat them in ways that would bring forth resistance in a saint.[12]

Even if the university is much better, the facts remain basically the same. A seminar at a university could be one of the highest forms of intellectual pleasure, but we must admit that it is mostly not so. I have just mentioned the basic principle, which Smothermon reveals is simply wrong. To elaborate the infinite implications is, of course, not possible without a further significant exploration. We are dealing

---

[11] Source of the quotation for certain reasons will be given only near the end of the work.

[12] Smothermon, Ron, *Play Ball, The miracle of children*, San Francisco, 1983, p.43.

with diverse, extremely subtle and traditional group dynamic mechanisms which would be an equally subtle art to uncover and put into language. Those who explore the future reaches of knowledge have always questioned – and ultimately debunked – the basic unconscious assumptions of which humanity is largely unaware, and which play an overwhelming main role in the human quagmire. The results of which will constitute the essential questions of future education[13] – provided that mankind decides to want to live on.

We initially misunderstood the instinct to play (which is learning) and, thus, slowly lost it. In the end, we impose it back on ourselves in a perverted form.

So perhaps my work might be called: "what I believe to have understood in Buddhism." If this sounds too childish for you, then that is exactly where the strength lies. A little more acceptable in court might be "The current state of my understanding of Chinese Buddhism." A consensus title might be: "What is Chinese Buddhism?"

I will try to answer this question on different levels – twice I found titles with the heading "The Flower of Chinese Buddhism" and "[History of] Chinese Buddhism" (the first book by Daisaku Ikeda and the other was a proseminar, which I could not attend but I had the documents given to me and it was divided into history, culture and theory). Theoria, from the Greek: the vision.[14] My primary interest is the vision. If I want to find out what Chinese Buddhism wants to say – culture and history are pushed into the background as outflows of the theory – I must take care of the

---

[13] The problem with the undiscovered is that there is no evidence of anything to uncover. We don't know that we don't know.

[14] Theoria comes from the Greek and is composed of theoros, the spectator and see. The literal meaning is to look at, examine, see as spectator.

vision. This work is devoted to the vision. Yes, this work is the attempt to present my vision of the Buddhist vision.

Sometimes a book is called a classic. In this vein, Erik Zürcher's "Buddhist conquest of China" is considered as such. Zürcher, from Leiden (Holland), is the only European specialist on Chinese Buddhism.

Chapter 1

Present Western Philosophy as an Introduction and Interpretive Basis for Chinese Buddhism

> But the only thing that a thinker can say, in each
> case, can neither be proved nor disproved logically
> or empirically. Nor is it a matter of faith. It can be
> seen through questioning and thinking. What is
> seen always appears as the questionable thing.[15]

1.1 The basic thesis

In Chris Bezzel's *Wittgenstein – Zur Einführung* (Wittgenstein – An Introduction) the following preface can be found, which shall also be valid as a basic thesis for my work:

> That neither philosophical New Academicism, nor Marxism, nor linguistics has yet adequately confronted the radical challenge posed by Wittgenstein, also certainly applies to this work.

I would like to expand here and say that this is true for the entire humanities and also, and especially true, for everyday communication. If I were an Indologist, a psychologist, an art historian, a sociologist or a German linguist my

---

[15] Heidegger, Martin; *Vorträge und Aufsätze*, Pfullingen, p.115.

master's thesis would – and this demands insight – begin with Wittgenstein. *The message to the world from Ludwig Wittgenstein has not yet been fully grasped.* This also applies to my subjects Sinology (Chinese), Philosophy and Religious Studies. From Wittgenstein:

> How does a person learn the meaning of the names of sensations? e.g. the word "pain." This is one possibility: words are combined with the original, natural, expression of the sensation and put in its place. A child has hurt himself, he cries; and now the adults talk to him and teach him exclamations and, later, sentences. They teach the child a new way of behaving with pain. "So you say that the word 'pain' actually means crying out?" – On the contrary; the verbal expression of "pain" replaces crying *and does not describe it.*[16]

The word 'pain' cannot represent the original sensation. Words cannot describe something in the sense of depicting it. The word "pain" is a verbal *interpretation* of the experience of pain. The pain itself is *pre-verbal*.

> A word cannot be true or false in the sense that it does not correspond to reality, or the opposite.[17]

Is this already a pain, or is this just very unpleasant? There is no objective boundary between "very unpleasant" and "already pain." Suppose you expose two people to the exact same "very unpleasant to pain stimulus." One may say

---

[16] Wittgenstein, Ludwig; *Tractatus logico-philosophicus*, Frankf../M., 1993, p.357.

[17] *ibid.* p.97 "Ein Wort kann nicht wahr oder falsch sein in dem Sinne, dass es nicht mit der Wirklichkeit übereinstimmen kann, oder das Gegenteil."

this is a pain, while the other will say this was very unpleasant. Two people use different words for the same sensation. However, it is also possible that the two do not have the same sensation at all. For one, perhaps the same stimulus triggers a different sensation than for the second. Furthermore, it would be possible that the one who is capable of feeling pain more strongly than the other is "tougher" and as a result will describe the sensation as merely "very unpleasant" while the other, because of his more sensitive predisposition, will experience the result of the stimulus as extremely painful. Because he is not so "tough" he will use the word "pain."

The words "pain" and "very unpleasant" are therefore not objectively measurable. The sensation is not objectively reproducible. The experience and the representation of the experience – the chosen word – are two separate areas. There is no mandatory voting rule between experience and the word chosen! There is no binding choice between sign and designated!

If you ask what pride is, for example, the answers go in two different directions. On the one hand, it will be expressed as conceit or conceitedness while, on the other hand, it might be expressed in the direction of dignity or dignified appearance. Nobody knows what "pride" is. Pride has no clear meaning. There is no pride *per se*. The word "passion" goes even more sharply in two completely different directions. So the "meaning" of a word can only be explained by other words, which in turn can only be explained by other words.

Does this also apply to the word "intuition"? How much more! The one considers intuition as an idea, the other one as a feeling, the third one quotes the 'definition' from the dictionary. The fourth even considers intuition to be a trait reserved for the female sex. If now a fifth would come and write out all "definitions" of intuition in the history of thinking of this world and say, here something shines through what intuition could really mean, then we would be closest to the matter.

But what if it is invalid not only for 'very unpleasant', 'pain' and 'intuition', but also for consciousness, atman, love, dialectic, freedom or substantiality? And it is true! The more abstract the words, the more it applies. What about for nirvana? Oh yes, it would be particularly so! Also for "Sunyata," the central word of Buddhism?

空

Actually, yes, but maybe we have a chance with this word that we don't have with other words.

> A sentence, a word has no meaning [...] given to it, as it were, by a power independent of us, so that one could make a kind of scientific investigation to find out what the word *really* means. A word has the meaning that someone has given it.[18] (emphasis mine)

and,

> We are unable to clearly circumscribe the terms we use; not because we do not know their real definition, but *because they have no real "definition."*[19] (emphasis mine)

With these characteristics, Western philosophy has come to its end. What Nietzsche had actually already ac-

---

[18] Bezzel, Chris; *Wittgenstein zur Einführung*, Hamburg, 1989, p.33.

[19] Schulte, Joachim; *Wittgenstein, eine Einführung*, Stuttgart, 1989, p.139.

complished (see below) is hereby sealed by Wittgenstein – the philosopher's only tool, human concepts, are indefinite and indeterminable quantities. Philosophy deals with undefined and indefinable things. One can give the terms definitions, but they don't have them by themselves, and that's the point. Wittgenstein explains:

> I can only name the objects. Signs represent them. I can only speak of them, I cannot express them.[20]

and,

> It is fundamentally impossible to make clear statements about our world; language fixes the world. The world, on the other hand, fluctuates and any attempt to represent the latter through the former only captures a fraction of one possibility.[21]

The world cannot be described, and the metaphysical world is all the more impossible to describe – which by no means says that you shouldn't try. The expressed word replaces. The word does not depict or represent it, but replaces or translates. Its replacing is, as we shall see, a creation. A language game is born.[22] With more subtle nuances, and when the nuances are mentally interpreted, a philosophy-language or a religion-language or another worldview-language replaces (translates) the actual experience. Philos-

---

[20] Wittgenstein, Ludwig; *Tractatus logico-philosophicus, Frankf./M.*, 1993, p.19 "Die Gegenstände kann ich nur nennen. Zeichen vertreten sie. Ich kann nur von ihnen sprechen, sie aussprechen kann ich nicht."

[21] Butzenberger, Klaus; *Einige Aspekte zur Catuscoti unter besonderer Berücksichtigung Nagarjunas*, p.9.

[22] Truly, the seemingly unphilosophical concept of "language game" is the key concept of Wittgenstein's entire philosophy. (Bezzel p.18).

ophy does not depict. It translates. Christian Morgenstern was even clearer than Wittgenstein, and said:

> Often I am suddenly overcome by a violent astonishment about a word. In a flash, the complete arbitrariness of the language in which our world is conceived and, thus the arbitrariness of our concept of the world in general, becomes clear to you. It was necessary to free the things from their arbitrary designation. To no longer take the word for the thing. To make clear the contradiction between being and naming.[23]

There is no binding choice between sign and what is signified! There is a relative relationship between sign and what is signified, and apart from apple and pear there is arbitrariness!! There is no definable word other than apple and pear. Nietzsche also saw that...

> ...the translation of nerve stimuli into images and of images into words is never natural, but rather is characterized by mere social agreements and arbitrary determinations.[24]

The Indian teacher of non-duality, Nisargadatta Maharaji, hits the nail on the head when he says "Names (in themselves) are empty shells."[25]

---

[23] Diary note read in the program "Lyrik nach Wunsch" on 1.9.96 in Radio Bayerischer Rundfunk 2.

[24] "Our whole philosophy is rectification of the use of language" (Nietzsche's reception of Lichtenberg), Martin Stingelin, Fink-Verlag, 1996, quote from Sueddeutsche Zeitung-Literatur, 6.11.96.

[25] Maharaj, Sri Nisargadatta; *Ich bin*, Bielefeld, 1988, p.208.

Sunyata

But is it not our opinion that gives *meaning* to the sentence? (And of course this includes: You can't mean meaningless rows of words). And meaning is something in the mental realm. But it is also something private! It is that intangible something; comparable only to consciousness itself.[26]

and,

"I'm not just saying this, I mean something by it." – If you think about what goes on in us when we *mean* words (and not just say them), it is as if something is coupled with these words, while they otherwise run empty – as if they intervene in us, so to speak.[27]

If they are *meant*, if they are coupled with something, they interfere with us. It can be that 'meant' words do not take hold in someone else's consciousness in the same way as in the consciousness of the speaker of these words. The person addressed does not understand what the speaker means.

The word also does not get its meaning from the context alone, but ultimately only from the recipient's state of consciousness.

When a word or phrase is held internally for a period of time and not mixed with other incidental material, it seems to infiltrate every part of our brain.... In our normal reading speed, such infiltration does not usually occur. But it does sometimes take place when one is reading the work of a great poet whom one particularly admires,

---

[26] Wittgenstein, Ludwig; *Tractatus logico-philosophicus*, Frankf../M., 1993, p.393.

[27] Wittgenstein, Ludwig; *Tractatus logico-philosophicus*, Frankf../M., 1993, p.434.

or the Bible, lingering over each word and giving it ample time. On such an occasion, one may read word by word, carefully and with great open-mindedness, and suddenly the passage will *seem charged with infinite meaning*, almost as if a revelation came from heaven. Anyone who has ever read the Bible with devotional piety must have had such an experience. We call this way of reading "language Samadhi," and this is what we must achieve when we recite a Zen-Koan. (Katsuki Sekida)[28]

The question, then, is what depth of feeling or insight the words strike, which string they hit, "how many parts of our brain are infiltrated."

The more intense the thought or desire, the more effective the preparation will be. Public announcements and ceremonies gather the thought, but the most effective amplifier of all is prayer or meditation. To be truly effective, a thought must be "determined, vividly conscious, *charged with* strongly felt good intentions, and steadily held for a long time."[29]

So the empty shells need to be "charged" to be effective. We have to put the "meaning" into the words. A word, itself, has no meaning. We *give* it meaning. Again, from Wittgenstein:

Our mistake is to look for an explanation there where we should see the facts as 'primordial phenomena'. i.e., where we should say: *this language game is played* (Tractatus S. 476).

---

[28] Powell, James N.; *Das Tao der Symbole – Vom wahren Wesen unserer Sprache*, München 1989, p. 130.

[29] *ibid*, p.190.

According to Wittgenstein, a religion, a philosophy, is a language game.

For hermeneutic research, religions are sign systems that interpret reality.[30] Does religion in and of itself perhaps represent a certain, peculiar kind of sign language? Religions would then be special languages to be learned.[31]

This is what Wittgenstein would refer to as a 'special language game'. So we can state a first intermediate result with certainty: Chinese Buddhism is the special language game "Chinese Buddhism." Chinese Buddhism thus falls into the area of which Wittgenstein said "my *whole* task consists in explaining the nature of the proposition."[32]

The problem of the humanities began more than a hundred years ago with the upswing and revolutionary enrichments of the so-called "exact sciences." Numbers and formulas may be exact, words *never* are. Words cannot be exact. It is too hard. No one wants to see it. When I told a (religious) physicist friend, who loves Kierkegaard and Pascal, that I now pursue religious studies as a second minor subject he only said ironically: "there you are. There's a science?"

The correct method of philosophy would actually be this: to say nothing but what can be said, i.e. propositions of natural science – that is, something that has nothing to do with philosophy – and then, whenever another wanted to say something metaphysical, to prove to him that he had not given any meaning to certain signs in his proposi-

---

[30] Waardenburg, Jacques; *Religonen und Religion*, Berlin, 1986, p.40.

[31] *ibid*, p.36 .

[32] Bezzel, Chris; *Wittgenstein zur Einführung*, Hamburg, 1989, p.57.

tions. This method would be unsatisfactory for the other – he would not have the feeling that we taught him philosophy – but it *would* be the only strictly correct one.[33]

Before I present my proposal of a new hermeneutic approach, I would like to analyze the old one with the following quotation:

> Hermeneutics, as the art of understanding what other people meant or mean, and "reading" their utterances, seems to be one of the basic concerns of the humanities.[34]

If only it was! I can in no way confirm that within university seminars in the humanities, the art of *understanding* an author is really a priority. The gap between mere knowledge and understanding (insight) is not presented to students at all. The word and the content are two different things. The "form vs. content" theme does not even emerge as such. The undisclosed form-fetishism is shocking, and clearly shows that we – as mankind – do not yet think. We mumble with forms, because the content does not open up to us. I don't want to offend anyone, but most people who do philosophy or religion (even those at university) make it clear by their being-so that they consider the word to be the content, more or less. Who has the courage to confess that he knows nothing? "No longer taking the word for the thing," as Morgenstern said earlier.

So I'll say it right away: The "scientific-ness" of the 'Humanities' is not a real criterion for me. Rather, the term "unscientific" would seem to me to represent a *higher* char-

---

[33] Schulte, Joachim; *Wittgenstein, eine Einführung*, Stuttgart, 1989, p.62.

[34] Waardenburg, Jacques; *Perspektiven der Religionswissenschaft*, Würzburg, 1993, p.124.

acteristic. Of course I know that the desire for clarity and, above all, for objectivity[35] is the motivating factor of such idolatry for this name.[36] But name worship is always a dead end. Best example for the entanglement is the so-called "science of religions":

> Rather, we make religion the object of research by distancing ourselves from it and objectifying it.[37]

"Distancing oneself" to gain a new perspective is fine, but "objectifying" it is not possible. A religious scholar himself once described this using a critical word:

> Those who have not experienced the *sacred* for themselves cannot understand what it is all about.[38]

It's not objectifiable. It cannot be objectified. It remains eternally subjective. It is not measurable and will, in all probability, remain un-measurable. This fact concerns not only the "sacred" but also the "beautiful," the "effectiveness," the "true," the "consciousness," the "art," the "love," the "achievement" or the "philosophy." We will never know what is the beautiful, the effectiveness, the true, the consciousness, the art, the love, the achievement or the philosophy simply because we do not have a valid yardstick to pin down these words. What "love" is remains un-measurable.

---

[35] That I share, and how I share it.

[36] Of the name "scientific."

[37] Waardenburg, Jacques; *Perspektiven der Religionswissenschaft*, Würzburg, 1993, p.98.

[38] Stolz, Fritz; *Grundzüge der Religionswissenschaft*, Göttingen, 1988, p.20.

So what is scientific work supposed to mean within the field of humanities? How can an insurmountable inaccuracy within humanities go together with the notion of a "science"? It's been just over 100 years since the concept of science was coined the "exact" sciences. From a psychological point of view, it doesn't actually mean anything different today than a sort of childlike emulation of a stronger big brother. The desire for clarity in the field of the humanities can only be realized with an admission of the impossibility of exactness and with an abandonment of the attachment to 'form'. What then is clarity? I would say it is a 'bringing to light'. But what is the 'light'? The strongest approach to this question is to repeat it: What is the light?

Language strives against its own limits by trying to say what is in reality beyond words. We "push against the limit of language," says Wittgenstein, "but the tendency, the push *points to something* ... I can only say that I do not disparage this human tendency; I take my hat off to it."

As Chuang Tzu (Zhuangzi) pointed out, this tendency of language to talk about things it basically cannot talk about is particularly evident in the subjects of philosophy and religion. Wittgenstein admits that his whole tendency "and I think the tendency of all people who ever tried to write or talk about ethics or religion was to run up against the limits of language. This running against the walls of our language is utterly, absolutely hopeless. In so far as it springs from the desire to say something about the ultimate meaning of life, the absolute good, the absolute value, ethics cannot be a science" […] We are constantly trying to twist and distort language to accomplish something that is not really its due. We talk about "love," "faith" and "God" − and yet these words have no fixed meaning. Everybody uses them differently. If everyone knows *the* meaning of the word "God," why do thousands of volumes have to be used for the arguments of theologians?

Why are Protestants and Catholics at war with each other in Ireland? Apparently, we can only converse with someone who uses the words in the same way we do. If someone plays the same game with the sound "God" as we do, then we can play along. Wittgenstein understood that it is useless to search for the meaning of a word. He explained that *the* meaning of a word lies in its use. We establish the meaning we want a word to have by the way we use it. A community is formed around words that are used in the same way by all of the community.[39]

The meaning of a word depends on its usage and just the valuable words like "soul" or "Spirit" or "intuition" or "being" are used by different thinkers and different traditions with somewhat completely different definitions and – what is the very cruelest – it is degraded again by our everyday consciousness anyway:

> When philosophers use a word – 'knowledge', 'being', 'object', 'I', 'proposition', 'name', – and seek to grasp the essence of the thing, one must always ask: Is this word ever actually used in this way in the language in which it has its home? *We* lead the words from their metaphysical, back to their everyday use.[40]

And a metaphysical meaning is not inherent in them either, except perhaps for the word "metaphysical."

A living thinker has called the 2500 years of philosophy as a kind of long-settled liberation movement. We have to say it has, by and large, failed and a philosophical culture has not emerged – not even a hint of philosophical experi-

---

[39] Powell, James N.; *Das Tao der Symbole – Vom wahren Wesen unserer Sprache,* München, 1989, p.132/133.

[40] Wittgenstein, Ludwig; *Tractatus*, Frankf../M., 1989, p.300.

ence of the world has prevailed.[41] This brings us to a new understanding.

1.2 Proposal of a hermeneutic approach

There were many outstanding thinkers. Karl Jaspers calls them authoritative people. Which approach is the most valuable? With which approach can the most be gained from a given text? Is it not urgent to ask this question? How can I benefit from thinkers? If I want to profit from them, is there any other way than to make an assumption from the outset that their thought trajectories are coherent. I make the following attempt: I take what they said from the outset at face value. I assume that what they claim is true and, from there, take a new look at the world and my life with the hypothesis of what they said. I take it as an opportunity to experiment whether their perspectives allow me to cultivate a more generous experience of the *conditio humana*. I pretend to believe. Does tentatively accepting a way of thinking expand my view of things? Does a space open up? Does an opening arise? Is there a clearing? Can I understand?

What experience might the writer have had that led him to use his special or unique verbalizations. So the quality that one would have to foster would be mental empathy. Unfortunately, general custom has always confused understanding with rational comprehension. This is where doom comes in at its root – the lower mind is a right/wrong machine. It examines things for compatibility with its own views and reacts accordingly with approval or disapproval. The pigeonholing into the approval/disapproval box is, in itself, already unintelligent. One projects their own world of

---

[41] That the history of the religions of the Occident is a history of failure is probably only not admitted by a few hardliners.

experience into the words of another and since the natural egocentricity is never aware of itself, only one possibility remains: What the other says is either right or wrong.

Add to this the innate joy of laryngeal activity, and the result is what is now called "discussion," from the Latin word *discutere*, "to sling around." Some people even consider themselves "intellectual." The real question is: Which form of 'thinking' enables me? What kind of thinking enables the true pleasure that is metaphysical? Which thinking makes love available?

If one wanted to trace back to when the word light was used for *insight*, the trail would probably get lost. Moreover, it seems to lie in the grounds of the soul that the person who gains insight wants to pass on his knowledge. To pass on 'understanding' would be the second point of this, "my" hermeneutic approach.

Is a 'content search' for light in texts possible? Is it possible to 'scan' for 'light' content? Unfortunately, it is not *objectively* possible. Whatever depth of insight or mental height one is able to project into a word like awareness, love or nirvana can hardly be influenced by the writer. The impact of the words, when read, depends on the recipient. The insight behind the words can be read out only if a correspondence is given to the reader within his own consciousness possibilities. Actually, it is read into it – equally read out and read in. Whoever reads, will always read from only their own state of consciousness or, at best, lightly polish it up. So one must almost say, philosophy is not communicable. We must be able to see the impossibility of philosophy to recognize its value.

1.3 The creation aspect of language

On the one hand, it is a matter of distinguishing between the sign and the signified. However, does the signified exist independently of the signification. Or does the word create the thing?

> No thing exists where the word is missing, namely the word that calls the thing forth in each case.[...] Only where the word is found for the thing, the thing is a thing.[42]

According to Heidegger, only the word provides the thing with existence. One can explain this with the example of the animal that is hungry. The animal is clearly hungry, but it has no word for hunger. Therefore, one cannot say that the animal is hungry. The animal has no awareness about its sensations. According to this thesis, awareness arises only through language. Only through language do things appear as things. Much could be discussed about this, but it would go beyond the scope of this present work. Nevertheless, I believe that it is so. The creation aspect of language is that reality is brought forth through it,[43] and only through it:

> Words do not label things already there. Words are like the chisel of the carver. They free the idea, the thing, from the general formlessness of the outside. As a man speaks, not only is his language in a state of birth, but also the very thing about which he is talking.

---

[42] Heidegger, Martin; *Unterwegs zur Sprache*, Pfullingen, p.163/4.

[43] Ultimately, it is not two aspects because the word, which can never depict, always brings forth something. There is no uncreative word, not even the curse. A curse is destructively creative.

Language is the bridge between the uncreated and the created...the ultimate reality, and the instrument by which reality is brought forth.[44]

Thus, two seemingly[45] irreconcilable discoveries about language are revealed: a) things only come into being through names and b) names are empty shells into which – in many cases, unfortunately – different "contents" (vibrations) are projected. I believe that both assertions are true. So it is correct to say in summary, as paradoxical as it is: *The vibration gives to the word its content, and the word to the vibration its existence.* So the meaning of a word is the vibration it is supposed to carry – emphasis on "supposed to" because it doesn't do it automatically. From another point of view, the vibration exists even without verbalization. But for man, this main principle applies that: "no thing exists where the word is missing" or "things are what the word makes of them by naming them."[46] Heidegger writes:

In every conversation and soliloquy there is an original translation.[47]

I could use this or that word to translate my state. The mood (vibration) itself is nameless. If I describe it as "gen-

---

[44] Erhard, Werner; from the prospectus for his then course "Communication: The power to accomplish, the power to relate," ca. 1986.

[45] Creme, Benjamin. "Growth of Consciousness," Lecture, Kerkrade, 18.Sept.1992.: "People cannot understand why two apparently opposite statements can coexist as truth. They do so because both of them are relative."

[46] Bailey, Alice; *Abhandlung über kosmisches Feuer*, Bietigheim, 1984, p.1119.

[47] Heidegger, Martin; *Parmenides*, Frankf../M., 1992, p.17.

tle bliss with some effort," it is "gentle bliss with some effort." If I describe it as "contentment based on achievement," it is "contentment based on achievement." But there is neither "gentle bliss with some effort" nor "contentment based on achievement." There is only experience translated into words and this is even more, exponentially more, true for philosophical experiences. I can <u>create</u> both "gentle bliss with some effort" and "satisfaction based on achievement" from a given mood.

One experiences a great liberation and exclaims, "God is dead." The other experiences a great liberation and exclaims, "I have experienced God." Wittgenstein doubles down:

> I could have expressed my experience of reading a word aptly in various ways by different words.[48]

Experience, in itself, is always nameless and is later translated into language. The moment of an experience of a word could be translated by Wittgenstein with another word, and just as well with a third (again other) word. Experience and verbalization of experience are the two separate realms of reality whose interaction to see through goes far beyond what is written here and is, in my opinion, *the* phenomenon of life par excellence.

When reading my own work, it is noticeable that I ecphore[49] other experiences with it at different times, so I do

---

[48] Wittgenstein, Ludwig; *Tractatus*, Frankf../Main, 1989, p.329 "Ich hätte mein Erlebnis beim Lesen eines Wortes auf verschiedene Weise treffend durch Worte ausdrücken können."

[49] A deeper explanation of this word will come in Section 1.5 but, essentially, it is the rousing of an engram or system of engrams from a latent to an active state (as by repetition of the original stimulus or by mnemic excitation).

not always read the same thing, even in my own sentences! My own sentences do not exist, even for me, "in themselves." They change, depending on how I look at them.

LEIDENSCHAFTLICH

4 MAL

From the miscellaneous remarks of Ludwig Wittgenstein (1931):

> That would be the end of a subject I don't know. It occurred to me today when I was talking about my work in philosophy and said to myself: I destroy, I destroy, I destroy...[50]

and,

> What I consider to be true, another may consider to be untrue; what is true for him is again false for me. So the meaning of statements are not yet firmly determined. The reason why they are not yet firmly determined is because I and the other (both) are biased.[51] [52]

---

[50] Wittgenstein, Ludwig; Über Gewissheit, Frankf../Main, 1994, p. 479.

[51] Even with great openness, we are "naturally-biased." Everyone's consciousness is pre-formed. There is no possibility for anyone not to pre-influence things through the filter of their own subjective consciousness

This means that I and the other associate different contents with one and the same "statement," i.e. that I and the other have (ecphore) different sensations by one and the same "statement." So there is no "statement" in itself. There can be no "statements" per se.

By way of anticipation, it should be noted here that the propositions of logic cannot be "thoughts" because they are tautologies or contradictions which say *nothing* because they do not represent anything.[53]

Language cannot represent. Always, all verbalizations (statements) remain tautologies. Every sentence, every philosophical statement, falls prey to the illusion that there is something to say, that a statement is possible. Testimony is not possible; in any case not a "correct" one.[54] A statement is always relative. An aphorism or a philosophy builds, with the first word, a coordinate system within which what is said is then seen as valid. Definition never defines itself out of itself; definition is always made, invented by man. According to Nietzsche, this is true even in mathematics (see

---

= Faxiang Buddhism (Yogacara) = modern neurobiology. This is how we create the world through our perception.

[52] Kempf-Bekkering, Friederike; *Der Kommentar Guo Xiangs zu den Kapiteln 1 und 2 des Buches Zhuang-zi*, p.94 (Master's thesis in sinology).

[53] Bezzel, Chris; *Wittgenstein zur Einführung*, Hamburg, 1989, p.75.

[54] A "statement" cannot be consistent or inconsistent. (A word cannot be true or false in the sense that it cannot correspond to reality, or the opposite). "Ein Wort kann nicht wahr oder falsch sein in dem Sinne, dass es nicht mit der Wirklichkeit übereinstimmen kann, oder das Gegenteil." Wittgenstein, Ludwig; *Tractatus logico-philosophicus*, Frankf../M., 1993, p.97.

quote about Aristotelian logic below). That is, a statement can only be consistent within a previously self-designed context of meaning. This, however, does not already exist by itself and is then represented by the human being. The context of meaning is designed by the human being. Another context of meaning could be designed and, in an instant, the supposed "statement" would become invalid. Thus, in the sense of the unconditionally enlightening awareness out of which this work[55] has been written, it can be said that every aphorism – every seemingly philosophical statement – could be seen as the repetition of the original aphorism of a Caesar who said "I came, I saw, I conquered." Which means nothing other than: I have interpreted the situation correctly and due to the coherence of my interpretation I have created from within my self-established system what I consider successful there.

> So I made a clear statement.
> I know something.
> There is something to say.
> What I say is the how I say it.
> I have put my stamp on life.
> I have meaning, or something has meaning.
> I am right.

In all this it has been forgotten that philosophy begins only when the philosophizer knows that he does not know.

---

[55] I think I know from which impetus Wittgenstein formulated his preface to the "Philosophical Remarks" and I would like to join in: "I would like to say 'this book is written for the glory of God', but that would be villainy today, that is, it would not be properly understood. It is said to be written in good will, and so far as it is not written with good will, that is, out of vanity, etc., so far the author would like it to be condemned. He cannot purify it further from these ingredients than he himself is pure from them." Schulte, Joachim; *Wittgenstein, eine Einführung*, Stuttgart, 1992, p.35.

The doer of the statement has forgotten that his subjective perception has always sent ahead of it its own original interpretation. The doer of a statement then pretends to negotiate something given. But this is not the case. He is already negotiating his pre-existing interpretation of things. With this insight we have worked out the most important 'message' of the Faxiang, the Chinese variant of the Indian Yogacara. I would like to say that this master's thesis is written in the Spirit of Faxiang Buddhism. Faxiang Buddhism is compressed in the Encyclopedia of Buddhism as follows:

> Everything is only ideation. Things exist only insofar as they are the content of consciousness.[56]

There is no experience of world without the filter of our own consciousness. We experience the world only as a product of our consciousness. Two neurobiologists (Maturana/Varela) have written a book which in its subtitle completely verifies the biological roots of human cognition. It is titled *The Tree of Knowledge:* **How we create the world through perception.**

A philosopher never interprets the world, but he always already interprets his subjective consciousness of the world. He interprets his own interpretation. There is no objective world out there to interpret at all, but he interprets what he has *created by his way of his own perception.*

The illusions (the relativity, the only conditional coherence) of the promulgations made by philosophers, scientists, gurus, politicians, sinologists, non-sinologists, scientific and less scientific sinologists are gathered in Caesar's Fundamental Saying (*veni vidi vici*) and laid bare in the above paragraph.

---

[56] *Lexikon des Buddhismus*, Bern, 1993, p.95.

Behind every "statement" is a big "so what." You can see it one way, but you can also see it another way. Everything that can be said can also be said differently. *Because language does not have the capability to depict*, it follows that the depiction can never be identical with what it claims to represent. That is, what is spoken does not exist at all. It originates in speaking!

This was also put forward from within a Heideggerian context:

> This is one of the greatest prejudices of Western philosophy: thinking has to be determined "logically," i.e. with regard to a statement.[57]

What is say-able, Heidegger calls the "saga":

> The saga cannot be captured in any statement.[58]

Thus, the tradition of thought[59] that places the greatest emphasis on the fact that its basic word is not a statement[60] stands out as one that withstand the current state of philosophy at its core.[61] An emphasis, when understood, comes to

---

[57] Heidegger, Martin; "Gesamtausgabe, 3. Abteilung: Unveröffentlichte Abhandlungen," *Band 65: Beiträge zur Philosophie* (Vom Ereignis), p.461.

[58] Heidegger, Martin; *Unterwegs zur Sprache*, Pfullingen, p.266.

[59] Buddhism, especially of the "Madhyamika" founded by the great Indian interpreter Nagarjuna (ca.150-250 A.D.), which is fundamental for the Sanlun, the Tientai, the Niutou and the Chan schools of Chinese Buddhism and is also the reference for the other Chinese Buddhist schools.

[60] Which, after all, would only be *one of several perspectives*.

[61] Cheng, Hsueh-li; *Nagarjuna's Twelve Gate Treatise*, Dordrecht, 1982, From the Introduction: "The hallmark of Madhyamika philosophy is

an end and – as we will see – no longer even appears as an emphasis. Jean Gebser states:

> All things, everything that one says, is always only partially correct. But it is important to say it in spite of the smile that arises inside about it; and it will be well said if something of these smiles also falls into the sentences. This does not always have to be the abrupt "but," or an "if," or a "because." Usually the order of the words is enough, which can make the sentence more thoughtful, or also a semicolon, or if it is a lot, a "so," which continues what has been started more carefully.[62]

So, with the spoken word, tone of voice, facial expressions, gestures, mimicry and volume are added as options – or irony, which increases awareness of what is only partially correct, expressing or referring back to everyday language. The written word does not have these options. It has, on the other hand, italics, capitalization, underlining, boldness, blocking and, more recently, font changes. I try to use these new possibilities to make certain sequences in my master's thesis more vivid.

The deliberate relativizations in my work – like "one could say" or "from a certain point of view" – are always full of intention.

The two European thinkers who triggered my sinology studies are at the same time the only ones I know who have already suggested a name for what comes after the end of philosophy:[63] The one, who originally brought me to sinolo-

---

'Emptiness', Sunyata. This is *not a view of reality. In fact it is emphatically denied that Sunyata is a view of reality.*"

[62] Gebser, Jean; *Gesamtausgabe Band.7*, Schaffhausen, 1980, p.252.

[63] Further suggestions can probably be found in the works of more recent thinkers.

gy with a philosophical assertion about the Chinese language (Arnold Keyserling), ends one of his books with:

> Thus, the new age demands an overcoming of philosophy by criticizing its premises, by determining the actual criteria of thinking: by creating the criteriology.[64]

Criterion is defined as: characteristic, distinguishing feature, identification mark.

My interpretation of this term: Previous philosophy has undiscovered features (premises and pre-existing biases). Their discovery would already be the criteriology.

That would mean the radical reinterpretation of the old philosophies in view of the "actual criteria of thought" to be found would be the criteriology. Criteriology would not be a "new kind of philosophy," but the working out of still unknown basic structures and biases of the handed down thought material.

Language never depicts facts. Language always conceptualizes. Philosophies are works of art which may well be compared with each other, but which above all stand next to each other once equally justified.

How does one receive art? In the best case, with correct resonance. As I said earlier in "Proposal of a hermeneutic approach," the most urgent question – actually, the *only* question – is what have I gained (as insight or true comprehension)?

---

[64] Keyserling, A.; *Der Körper ist nicht das Grab der Seele, sondern das Abenteuer des Bewusstseins*, Verlag Im Waldgut, 1982, p.67.

1.4 The current state of Philosophy through Jean Gebser's cultural analysis

This fundamental transformation of philosophy, which aims at its own overcoming, is not only evident in Heidegger. If we follow this tendency of the philosophical schools of our days in general, it becomes apparent that the space-restricted, conceptual-bound thinking of the rational kind begins to give way to a new mode of re-alization whose characteristics are quite **aperspectival** (see ff). These approaches to overcoming the three-dimensional mentality in philosophy and thus to their own overcoming express themselves as follows:

1. incorporating "time" as an element of its own in philosophical thinking.

2. in the admission of the inadequacy of the rational.

3. in the turn towards the whole and to diaphaneity. (= transparency = shining through of the Spiritual)[65]

It would be quite easy to prove that Gebser (1905-1973) summarizes here quite aptly the signs of the present as he represents in general, with his view and analysis of the history of our genre. He is probably the most spacious European mind of the 20th century.[66] Because of his overview

---

[65] Gebser, Jean; *Gesamtausgabe 3*, Schaffhausen, 1978, p.544.

[66] His panoptic and interlinking nature in thought showed itself also in the friendship and/or acquaintance with essential figures of the European intellectual history of the 20th century like Lorca, Picasso, C.G. Jung, Heisenberg, Lama Govinda and also the contact to Asia. While C.G. Jung avoided the direct personal meeting with Ramana Maharshi last-minute, Gebser looked for the human encounter. So he led conversations with the vice president of India, at that time Radhakrishnan,

of most disciplines of human endeavor, he will perhaps one day be called the last universal scholar.[67] I always marvel at how this man had the genius – out of the short time within his century – to grasp, to elaborate and to clarify the dimension of the turning point of time at which we are standing with such clarity of broad, content-dense, concise concepts.[68] Partly coined by himself, he divides the walking of man on earth into five great states of consciousness, which came about through long-lasting mutations: the archaic, the magical, the mythical, the mental and now the integral consciousness. The five stages become clear – e.g. in their relation to the ratio of the ability to reason. The archaic had of course no relation to any ratio of reasoning, the magical could be called pre-rational. The mythical age was also still irrational, while the mental finally brought the breakthrough to the rational. Now, at the transition into the integral age, the leap into the arational consciousness is waiting. Arational means above all not unrational, but supra-rational or overrational. The main characteristic of the integral world is – as the name suggests – the inclusion of all previous mutations of consciousness. In relation to the ratio, this means that it is available in the integral being as a play type at any time. In other words, the supra-intellectual has integratedly left behind the stage of the intellectual.

---

with D.T. Suzuki, with Gopi Krishna and visited several ashrams; among others, those of Ramana Maharshi and Sri Aurobindo.

[67] He was also the one who, with his statements about the importance of meeting China via his book *Asien lächelt anders*, brought me back to the study of Sinology after initial failed attempts and foreign courses.

[68] Here, too, the following applies: There is no such thing as exactness in the humanities. See also Chapter 5.3.

According to Gebser, the last mutation (from the mythical to the mental) took place around 500 B.C. through figures like the Pre-Socratics, Socrates and Plato in Greece; Buddha or Mahavira in India; Laozi (Lao-tse) and Kongzi (Confucius) in China. At that time, philosophy replaced mythology. Today, philosophy is replaced by "Eteology." The eteologem will thus replace the philosophem. For example, "methods" or "systems" of philosophy in which some still place hope, and whose limitations are analogous to the term "scientificity," may well shine through in my writing and belong (according to Gebser) to the old age.

One of Gebser's basic words that appear in his main work as a heading for the new age is **aperspectival**. Previous philosophy was, in stark terms, just perspectives. But we are now on the way to the aperspectival world. What Gebser experienced, what led him to his formulations, the wide awake[69] reader of his books will be able to understand. Thus Gebser was allowed to subtitle his main work *Origin and Presence*[70] with justification, *Manifestations of the Aperspectival World*. The aperspectival world is thus the overthrow of the previous merely perspectival approaches to the world. Access to this world is:

> …The diaphanon, the open, the Spiritual true as World-Verition: the world perceived and imparted in truth.[71]

What is at stake is the level of insight that drove Gebser to these terms. That is, the intellectual-historical

---

[69] also a word he likes to use.

[70] *Ursprung und Gegenwart* – English title: "The Ever-present Origin."

[71] From the Synoptic Table to his main work "Ursprung und Gegenwart" (engl. "The Ever-present Origin"), *Gesamtausgabe 2/3*, Schaffhausen, 1978.

context within which he wants these words to be understood. This is described as...

> ...diaphanous, achronic, time-free rendering of the ever-present origin of the whole.

In integral, aperspectival consciousness is primarily about the whole.[72] Here, Buddhism will have much to say to us. The integrating diaphanous is always also a stepping out of time. Here Gebser makes an essential distinction between timelessness and time-freedom. He attributes timelessness to the deficient magical epoch. Time-freedom, the "fourth dimension," is what will constitute the emerging new structure of consciousness. Time-freedom can only be achieved by those who have managed to control time and can then escape from its grip. Gebser uses as a collective term "arational, achronic awareness" – perhaps more commonly translated as "supra-rational, time-independent awareness." His words get their meaning from his state of awareness. His state of awareness seeks to convey itself through the context he creates in his books. The context-raising of Gebser's work is currently (for now) the truest dimension in which words can take place. So I choose his context as context for my writing. This master's thesis is written after the end of philosophy. This master thesis is written at the end of the old age. Its motivation aims at anchoring-in the supra-intellectual, the supra-rational. One of its questions is: what

---

[72] What is the whole? The whole is the whole. The whole is the thought of what is to think as "the whole." The whole is probably the <u>idea</u> of "the whole." A rather significant idea: Even if there were two universes completely separated from each other, it would still be a whole with two parts! "What is one is one. What is not one is also one." Chuang Tzu (Zhuangzi).

In Fromm, Erich (D.T. Suzuki, R. de Martino); *Zen-Buddhismus und Psychoanalyse*, Frankf../M., p.131. "Nothing that is not part of the whole, i.e., anything that is different is the different from the same!"

part of the previous philosophy can be saved over into the new era. Buddhism offers a lot here.

I believe that "direct intuition" is the most apt expression for the new mode of realization towards which the pioneering, groundbreaking work of Jean Gebser is heading.[73] In order to give an impression of what "direct intuition" is, I would like to describe how it completely gripped me for the first time. In the explosion of consciousness phase which occurs in late puberty, I wanted to know everything about the "Spiritual world," the philosophers, etc. It was only when I, as with every name that happened to me, looked up "Anthroposophy" a moment of complete realization arose: "that's it!"

> Anthroposophy teaches that every human being can recognize the higher worlds present in him, if he only awakens the cognitive abilities slumbering in him for this purpose. […] Rudolf Steiner believed to have come to such a state of insight. According to this, the earth develops from an initially purely Spiritual state through seven stages of increasing materialization back into its original state. The development of man corresponds to this development, indeed it depends on the development of man whether the earth will return to its original Spiritual state.[74]

It was a complete realization. The re-spiritualization of matter is the process which takes place. Direct intuition says "it cannot be anything else." The "Spiritualization of matter" is really what it's all about. "Direct intuition" unlocks truth without reasoning. Only with direct intuition one can

---

[73] Being directly intuitive can only be claimed by someone who has demonstrated rational astuteness. One cannot skip one level.

[74] *Lexikon 2000*, Bd.1, Stuttgart, 1970, p.333.

speak of philosophical certainty. Only direct intuition knows. Direct intuition has no doubt that "world" means "re-spiritualization of matter."

> There is no other insight than an intuitive one. Deduction and discourse, falsely called findings, are only instruments leading to intuition. As soon as this is reached, the means used for it disappear before it; in cases where it cannot be reached, reasoning and discourse remain like signposts pointing to an intuition out of reach; when it has finally been reached, but is not a present mode of my consciousness, the maxims of which I avail myself remain as results of operations previously performed, as what Descartes called "recollections of ideas." And if one asks what intuition is, Husserl will answer, in agreement with the majority of philosophers, that it is the presence of the "thing"[75] in consciousness.[76]

1.5 Hypothesis on the foundation of philosophy

One of the strengths of American thinking is its practical psychology orientation; one wants to know how the psyche functions in order to be able to exploit the "human potential." In German-speaking countries, the Swiss man Josef Hirt had a similar approach with his "Law of Lust and Unlust." Every sensation leaves an engram[77] in the mneme

---

[75] Or better: Insight into the "thing," or idea of the "thing," which means the actual "thing," but this is not experienced with general-unphilosophical world perception. The general world perception is therefore the world false perception.

[76] Sartre, Jean-Paul; *Das Sein und das Nichts*, Hamburg, 1995, p.324.

[77] An "engram" refers to the enduring offline physical and/or chemical changes that were elicited by learning and underlie the newly formed

(the persistent or recurrent effect of past experience of the individual or of the race). By endogenous or exogenous stimuli, old engrams are permanently revived. This is called ecphoria (verb: to ecphore). We never experience in an unbiased manner because old engrams are automatically revived – ecphored, as soon as we register a similarity with something known. The resuscitation process of old engrams is always triggered in response to the felt similarity of the respective most emotional engram that is ecphored, because the consciousness strives primarily for intensity (only *primarily*! See 3.1.3). All this is subject to the Law of Lust and Unlust.[78] The human computer works according to a pattern – avoid unlust in favor of lust. The common distinction between pleasure principle and achievement principle does not apply, because the achievement principle is chosen since its result is the more long-lasting strategy to avoid feelings of unlust. The achievement principle is the application of the fundamentally valid Law of Lust and Unlust. Thinking, for Hirt, is the process of ecphoria and association, and it *must* strive for Lust. For Wittgenstein, it is:

> Peace in the thoughts. This is the desired goal of the one who philosophizes.[79]

---

memory associations. "Engram cells" are populations of cells that constitute critical cellular components of a given engram.

[78] According to Hirt: The feeling of displeasure associated with the sensation of the child falling into the water is so dominant at the moment that it blindly activates to the saving act. The human being is completely subject to one single law: He must avoid displeasure and strive for lust; all considerations for a functioning ethics can only be gained on this background.

[79] Bezzel, Chris; *Wittgenstein zur Einführung*, Hamburg, 1989, p.44.

The connection of sensation and word (as we saw with Morgenstern and Nietzsche: almost arbitrary!!) is supposed to be lustful. It was lustful (peaceful) for Kant to formulate that we humans can never reliably look behind the veil of space and time, that we will never know the "thing in itself." For Nietzsche, it was lustful (peaceful) to title man's response to his exposure with the essence "will to power." The "translation of nerve stimuli into words" strives for that formulation which appears most lustful to the consciousness bearer concerned (do not misunderstand the Law of Lust and Unlust now – complex facts can only be expressed in complex words). That the "translation of nervous stimuli into words" **must be lustful** could be recognized as the *source* of poetry, philosophy and religion. The *German Compendium on the History of Chinese Thought* was published as *China and the Hope for Happiness.*[80]

Packaging experience in abstraction is lustful. Abstraction and naming abstraction are two different things. One thinker with relatively similar experiences as another gives his abstractions different names and the more abstract the more valid:

> ...it is well nigh impossible to resolve abstractions into the terms of speech, and not lose the inner sense in the process.[81]

If one philosopher interprets the other, he can only misunderstand him because it is to be excluded that he

---

[80] Bauer, Wolfgang; *Paradiese, Utopien, Idealvorstellungen in der Geistesgeschichte Chinas*, München, 1989. (*China and the Search for Happiness*, "Recurring Themes in Four Thousand Years of Chinese Cultural History," N.Y., 1976.)

[81] Bailey, Alice; *Abhandlung über kosmisches Feuer*, Bietigheim, 1984, p.663.

could ecphore the same experiences with all names. We never experience thoughts on a purely intellectual level, but always with additionally triggered sensations. Our thinking is *thought-feeling.*[82]

> The philosophical problems are misunderstandings, which are to be eliminated by clarifying the rules according to which we want to use words.[83]

In a certain sense, Sigmund Freud was perhaps the most thorough thinker there has been, because he really went to the base foundation of man.[84] In his succession, thinkers (psychoanalysts, and those of the more advanced schools) emerge. They are the realists among philosophers – they see man as what he really is, a big grown baby (perhaps the only interpretation-free fact about us) who in an older language are called children of God. Two of them write:

> Affects are the primary data of psychoanalysis and they give words their meaning. They are the carriers of the semantic content. If one assumes that the communication and non-communication of affects gives the communicated words their meaning, much clarifies itself as if by itself.[85]

---

[82] That is, in the better case. More strictly analyzed, it is thought-feeling only in rare cases. Mostly it is thought-emotion, in that feeling is the more subtle and emotion the cruder. See on this in the chapter "The Crisis of established (secure) knowledge."

[83] Bezzel, Chris; *Wittgenstein zur Einführung*, Hamburg, 1989, p.45.

[84] His fatal weakness, however, is that he did not go up. He did not have the faintest concept of our higher (spiritual) nature.

[85] Model, Arnold, H; in: Psyche, *Zeitschrift f. Psychoanalyse*, Stuttgart, März 1984, p.222.

and,

> Since thinking is an unconscious mental activity whose locus is similar to the relationship between baby and breast, we can recognize the combined primal object, breast and nipple, as the actual source of knowledge. Inner teaching means that the breast knows everything in a categorical sense. It is omniscient, containing all knowledge – not in terms of external reality, of course, but as a category of meaning in psychic reality. The words given by external objects as empty containers are filled with meaning only by the inner breast. But this is a lifelong process by which experience can be assimilated so that the verbal categories of the ever-progressing stages of abstraction are filled with meaning. Filling old words with new meaning ....[86]

Whether 'freedom', 'love', 'happiness', 'beauty', 'life', 'friendship', 'relaxation', 'money', 'joy' – they all mean mother's milk. An assertion which is, according to Wittgenstein's philosophy of language, only a minor consequence.

'Transcendence', 'idea', 'being', 'Tao', 'nothing', 'truth', 'pneuma' (the gnostic Spirit-soul), 'noosphere' (Teilhard de Chardin), 'Self', 'metaphysics', 'logos', 'monad', 'beautiful spark of God' are the particular words that insist on *not* meaning mother's milk. We must give them a chance. It is said that everything that is, is somewhere in the tension between Spirit and matter. We are "Spirit immersed in matter." In fact, it is often pointed out that matter comes from Latin *mater*, the mother. So the words that insist on not meaning mother's milk must mean the opposite pole, which is usually called "Spirit" in German. What is "Spir-

---

[86] Meltzer, Donald; *Traumleben, Überprüfung der psychoanalytischen Theorie und Technik*; München, 1988, p.121.

it?" One could say that in German Spirit (Geist) is what Hegel said of it, for he is known to have strained this word like no one else. And so he is synonymous with the optimal updating of this word. It has forced itself on me to baptize those words, which insist on not meaning mother's milk, as father's-milk-words. The mother's milk is given – the father's-milk we have to create. It exists, but only if we recreate it does it become accessible to us.

Language strives against its own limits by trying to say what is, in reality, beyond words. We "push against the limit of language," says Wittgenstein, "but the tendency, the push, *points to something*...." (emphasis mine).

All philosophy, all religion, points to...the father's-milk. All philosophy, all religion, has the task to "bring over" the milk of the father.

Two of the essential (for many, the two *most* important)[87] Western philosophers of the 20th century arrive at the formulation of quite different trajectories of thought:

---

[87] I think you can basically observe two kinds of philosophy. One is the type that weaves webs with thought matter, people who are good with thought verbalizations and experience thought matter in a very concrete way. The other is the type that wants to approach "metaphysical Events" in a more direct way. Weakness of the former is verbosity, clarity is not the primary goal. They briefly open one room and then close two. Weakness of the latter is that they recognize something they find difficult to formulate. Among them are Heidegger and Wittgenstein. Interestingly, they both admitted to being a stutterer. (Heidegger: *Aus der Erfahrung des Denkens*, p.121; Wittgenstein: *Über Gewissheit*, p.476).

My affinity is with the stutterers. Roughly speaking, in European terms, the former are the French, the latter the Austrians and Germans. Buddhism as such is the most mature form of 'direct' approach. Chinese thought, as such, is of the other approach in its 'worldliness'. Chinese Buddhism is a synthesis of the two fundamentally different approaches to philosophy.

Philosophy should actually only be written in poetry.[88]

and,

The poetic character of thought is still hidden. Where it shows itself, it is for a long time like the utopianism of a half-poetic intellect.[89]

It could be summarized: The philosophers (and the religious thinkers) were all 'only' the better poets.

The present state of Western philosophy is that many believe that it still exists, and those who know that it has dissolved are not serious about the consequences.

But it will return purified. Similarly, as Nietzsche said, "the moral God is dead, but he will return flayed as God beyond good and evil." So, according to Heidegger:

The metaphysics that has been overcome does not disappear. It returns transformed and remains in control as the ongoing distinction between being and the essent (the existing).[90]

What the difference of being to essent (the existing) – the so-called ontological difference – is why it is so crucial, and we will come to see later in this work what all this has to do with Chinese Buddhism. For skeptics, it could be said it is Buddhism if we can assume that Buddhism is its content and not its name.

[88] Bezzel, Chris; *Wittgenstein zur Einführung*, Hamburg, 1989, p.56.

[89] Heidegger, Martin; *Gesamtausgabe 13*, Frankf../M., p.84.

[90] Heidegger, Martin; *Vorträge und Aufsätze*, Pfullingen, p.68.

1.6 The overhaul of Aristotelian logic

> For Western thinking, Aristotelian logic was valid (at least until recently): It is based on the theorem of identity (A=A), on the theorem of contradiction (A is not non-A), and on the theorem of the excluded third party (A cannot be both A and non-A, and neither A nor non-A). In contrast to Aristotelian logic is the so-called paradoxical logic, which assumes that A and non-A are not mutually exclusive as predicates of X. Paradoxical logic prevailed in Chinese and Indian thought....[91]

Already Nietzsche 'gnawed' at the foundations of Aristotelian logic:

> We fail to affirm and deny the same thing: this is a subjective sentence of experience, no "necessity" is expressed in it, *but only a non-capability.* If, according to Aristotle, the *proposition of contradiction* is the most certain of all principles, [...] All the more carefully one should consider what *assertions* he basically *presupposes.* Either something is asserted with regard to the real, the being, as if one already knew it from somewhere else; namely, that no opposite predicates *can* be attributed to it. Or the proposition wants to say: that opposite predicates *should not* be attributed to it. Then logic would be an imperative *not* for the knowledge truth, but for the setting and rectification of a world *which we want to call true.* In short, the question is open: are the logical axioms adequate to the real, or are they standards and means to create the real, the concept of "reality" for us in the first place? ... In order to be able to affirm the first, one would have to, as I said, already know the being; which is absolutely not the case. Thus, the proposition does not

---

[91] Fromm, Erich (D.T. Suzuki, R. de Martino); *Zen Buddhismus und Psychoanalyse,* 1981, p.131.

contain a criterion of truth, but rather an imperative about *what should be considered as true*. If such a self-identical A did not exist at all, as every proposition of logic (also of mathematics) presupposes, the A would already be *apparent,* then logic would presuppose a *merely apparent* world. [...] Our belief in things is the prerequisite for the belief in logic. [...] By not grasping this and making logic a criterion of "true being," we are already on the way to considering all those hypostases: 'substance', 'predicate', 'object', 'subject', 'action' as realities....[92]

We *set* them as realities! So that A is not not-A, A must be set as A *beforehand*. This setting, this definition is not given by nature, it is – rigorously stated – the free invention of Aristotle. This is not to devalue the invention, but it is to show that it *is* an invention. If it were clear anyway that A is equal to A, would one have to make a principle out of it? It is not clear, that A must first be declared to be A. Today we know that everything is in constant flux. In order to explain that A is A, it already takes the artificial process of fixation – which only occurs by a certain use of time functions (how long then does A, remain A?).

> The logic only applies to fictitious truths that we have created. It is the attempt to comprehend the real world according to a scheme of being set by us, more correctly, to make it formulable, calculable for us. It refers to our ideas, in so far as they correspond to our imaginative faculty and not, in so far as they correspond to an intrinsic reality.[93]

---

[92] Nietzsche: "Der Wille zur Macht," Stück Nr.516, quoted from: Volkmann-Schluck, K.-H., *Interpretationen zur Philosophie Nietzsches,* Frankf../M., 1968, p.92

[93] Nietzsche, in: *Klassiker der Philosophie, Bd.2,* München, p.215.

Nietzsche exposed logic as inadequate, and Heidegger's familiar style exhibited the same landmark characteristics:

> Thinking begins only after we have learned that reason, which has been glorified for centuries, is the most persistent adversary of thinking.[94]

The sacred cows of Western thought, Aristotelian logic and the single-layered concept of reason,[95] are thus outdated. Against it is:

> Paradox, a basic concept of the aperspectival world.[96]

A sinologist has written out in a fundamentally explanatory manner what is quickly intuited by many young people and, who might never have heard of Spirit other than in the atmosphere of the New Time, quickly lights up without the need of much explanation:[97]

> In Buddhist literature we find statements that appear to say 'X is not X' or 'there is no X', and by literalist interpretation these are all too easily misconstrued as paradoxical, illogical, or simply nonsensical. Sometimes they are considered a kind of shock treatment; though this may be one of their functions, they are not so limited, provided further thought is applied. What these statements present, besides a challenge to fixed conceptions, is a shift in per-

---

[94] Heidegger, Martin; *Holzwege*, Frankf../M., 1994, p.267.

[95] The word "reason" from a completely different point of view in the paragraph "The crisis of established (secure) knowledge" (Chapter 5).

[96] Gebser, Jean; *Gesamtausgabe Bd.7*, Schaffhausen, 1978, p.300.

[97] Basically, more than "quickly" – just *directly*, that is, *immediate*.

spective. A statement which appears to say "X is not X" may mean "the conventionally agreed upon idea of a phenomenon labeled X is not the ultimate essence or reality of X," or "the temporary phenomenon called X is not an enduring self-subsistent X," or "the concept conventionally associated with the name X is not itself an objectively real phenomenon of which the name X is an inherent property." Similarly, "there is no X" may mean "there is no permanent, objective reality which ineluctably corresponds to the idea associated with the name X," or simply "there is no permanent X" or "there is no self-defined X," or *names do not correspond to realities*," or "things are not what we think they are."[98] (emphasis mine)

The appeal of Buddhism to the modern Western thinker who is just coming up to speed now should tend toward "irresistible," for there was no Aristotle in the Buddhist world. "Names do not correspond to realities" is the most urgent correspondence of Wittgenstein with Buddhism, or at least parts of Buddhism, where writers who fall under "Buddhism" are aware of the above. Indeed, much has been written about the Wittgenstein/Buddhism parallels. I (and many others) consider this a crucial track of contemporary philosophical thought.

---

[98] Cleary, Thomas; *Entry into the Inconceivable, Introduction into Hua-Yen Buddhism*, Honolulu, 1983, p.18.

65

Chapter 2

The Deep Structure of Chinese Buddhism

缘起　二言帝　空

Yuanqi　　　　Erdi　　　　　Kong

Religions are poems,
They bring our daytime and dream Spirit into harmony,
our feelings, instincts, breath and innate gestures into the
only perfect thinking: poetry
[…]
Full religion is the great poem in loving repetition
[…]
flashing in a flexible manner we call it poetry
anchored around a center we call it religion
[…]
There will always be religion as long as there is poetry, or
a lack of it
[…]

Les Murray

2.1 The discriminating thought operation of Buddhism: Yuanqi

> Buddhism claims that language has no ontological meaning. A word does not correspond to a part of reality. Words are nothing but signs invented for everyday use and have nothing in common with the structures of reality. A word is nothing but an unfounded construct *whose meaning is determined only by its relation* to other words.[99]

The assertion that the context determines the "definitions" implies the irresolvable difficulty that the context is in turn composed of words that can only be defined by other words. A dictionary defines words by other words, which in turn are defined by other words.

Meanwhile, modern linguistics since Ferdinand Mongin de Saussure (1857-1913) has also clearly grasped this: Signifiers are not defined by signifieds, but by other signifiers, i.e. a word cannot define itself by its content, or its meaning, but by a word similar to it. Thus, a word cannot define itself by what it is supposed to mean, because that remains intangible.

In essence, there is only one unknowable single web of words that owe their identity to their demarcation from other words. The word does not exist independently of others because it is defined by what it is not. When I say a single word, I am mainly saying that it is not all the others.

There is no sign that has meaning on its own.[100]

---

[99] Izutsu, Toshihiko; *Philosophie des Zen-Buddhismus*, Hamburg, 1986, p.72.

[100] Bezzel, Chris; *Wittgenstein zur Einführung*, Hamburg, 1989, p.52.

That Saussure made it clear before Wittgenstein, so Chris Bezzel from the very outset was wrong to say,

> That neither philosophical New Academicism, nor Marxism, nor linguistics have yet adequately confronted the radical challenge posed by Wittgenstein is considered certain for this work.

Linguistics did make it clear! So, first the Buddhists explained it, then Saussure, then Wittgenstein.[101] The network of words is such that each word derives its identity solely from its differentiation from other words, so only the network exists as a whole. The assertion that only the network as a whole exists is already an application of Yuanqi. But it can also be derived from the previous sentence, "There is nothing that is not part of the whole, that is, NOTHING is different from the one." If thought through to the end, one word is all words.[102]

What is not said is also said, because with one word all others are always already mentioned. What I mean to say here, of course, is that it is only true on the abstract level. In both Latin (*abstrahere*) and Chinese (*chouxiang*) the words for 'abstract' literally mean "pull out."

The abstract is the "essence" drawn out. The abstract as "pulled out" essence is, thus, actually the most tangible.

---

[101] In my next book I will present a little-known tradition of thought where a word has an equivalent in reality – something which at this moment in Planetary Wisdom lore seems to be impossible. So far a word can not apply to reality. But wait for my next and last book. There is an exact humanities. There is an exact Spiritual science. There is exact terminology. **[See also important additional note on page 249]**

[102] That is why the ancient Indians say there is only one word: The OM. For Heidegger: Every word (is), as a word, a word of 'Being'. For the Bible: In the beginning was the Word (not the words).

抽象

The 'stupid', most disastrous thing is already apparent here: that our words for "abstract" are themselves again pictorial ideas derived from the physical level. But what if the abstract is precisely the non-pictorial, and the image of the 'extracted essence' is already only a bad paraphrase for what abstraction means? Ultimately it doesn't apply because the abstract is not physical, not formal, and is virtually insubstantial. Perhaps abstractions can be described as non-forms. You can't understand them. Abstract means formless. The abstract and the concrete become one another and will always bite each other! The abstract and the concrete are not equivalents on the same level. The abstract and the concrete are not equivalent! The abstract stands above the concrete! The abstract has the task of abstracting from the concrete, to filter out the essence from the concrete. To abstract means to make essences – which are actually "insubstantial" – substantial. To think abstractly means to be able to grasp insubstantialities and to work with them.

However, the current language with its 'lousy' imagery is a degrading means for expressing rigorously abstract thought. Not even the word 'abstraction' can say what it means!

The closest way we can reach a word is by circling it, and by separating it from those words closest to it. A word is defined by the fact that it is not a word similar to it. The word "consciousness" is easy to distinguish from the word "thought," or the word "philosophy" from the words "knowledge" or "insight." They can also be separated relatively clearly.

Chouxiang
"Abstract"

Perhaps "awareness" comes closest to "consciousness." "Awareness" would then, above all else, not be "consciousness." Awareness separates itself from consciousness, knowledge, wisdom, self-consciousness, intelligence, insight.

Nowhere – neither in the visible nor in the invisible world – is there such a thing as an area which on the front displays an inscription which says "Intelligence," and then the door opens and inside is "Intelligence." The word "intelligence" is a paraphrase that describes something indefinable. The paraphrase is not clearly definable in a manner that one could then say this is "intelligence," but it is not "insight," etc.

There are no *things* such as awareness, consciousness, knowledge, wisdom, consciousness, intelligence or insight that can be clearly identified or contained. There are only words, which can carry a certain vibration or not. Wittgenstein claims that there is not even an "aura which the word brings with it and takes over in every use."[103] I would like to contradict that statement here to some extent: The *aura* of "awareness" is clearly not the aura of "apple," "courage," or "desire." But the auras of consciousness, knowledge, cognition, wisdom, awareness, intelligence, insight, attention or alertness do intermingle a lot. So the aura of "awareness" is not the aura of "apple," "courage," or "wish" and *especially* not the aura of consciousness, knowledge, cognition, wisdom, intelligence, insight, finding, attention, alertness.

The near impossibility of communicating philosophy needs to be confronted. Insight is virtually incommunicable because with the same words the listener does not have the same sensations (auras) as the speaker. Strictly speaking, this is true for every conversation except in geometry, arithmetic, chemistry, etc.

---

[103] Bezzel, Chris; *Wittgenstein zur Einführung*, Hamburg, 1989, p.33.

If words had clear meanings, then the only correct interpretation of a text would be to reproduce it as it stands, i.e. to copy it word for word or to read it down verbatim. The change of a single word would be inadmissible.

When an eastern or western philosopher – religiously inclined or not – says, for example, "The truth is the whole" not only is one word explained by another, it is equated with it. The objection would be "the true is the true, and the whole is the whole." Point taken. If the true is the true, then it cannot be the whole and vice versa. If words are seen as substantial then such an equation is inadmissible.

Here is illustrated the impotence of language for philosophy – the cat bites its own tail. Those who have observed this phenomenon closely know that the cat is not aware that it is chasing its own tail. It thinks "someday I will catch this thing" because it does not know that it is her own tail. This is an exact analogy to human language in philosophizing. The philosopher explains one word by another, or by a certain stringing together of several words, or he explains several words by a few compact ones. Then the word is defined in a compact manner. But the word does not have this compactness in itself. All philosophy is a cat-tail mess.

What is a chapter? One word or few words are prefixed compactly as a heading and then the one word is explained by many words. The many words, from which the one word is uniquely different, must now serve to explain the one compact word. We are already back to poetry. Compact, concentrated, dense words are poetry. Seen in this way, the heading of a chapter is always poetry.

The difference between the two words above (true and whole) is that no one knows what the "true" thing is while the "whole" sounds quite conceivable.

Yuanqi
"dependent co-arising"
"existence only by mutual evocation"

Chinese philosophical tradition makes use of a term called the "net of words." According to this tradition, the best statement is one that does not "fall into the net of words."[104]

Such a statement should actually be impossible and yet I did it towards the end of my remarks. It makes no sense anymore to philosophize around using ambiguous tools (man-made terms which, after all, only represent human limitation). Therefore, as Heidegger said, the danger of thinking is philosophizing.[105]

So we ask for a concept that is realistic, the whole. The whole is the whole. The whole is everything. With the term "everything" we can be allowed to philosophize because "everything" is a clear term. "Everything" is simply everything. Perhaps "everything" is the only unambiguous word besides apple and pear. Let us take "all" instead of "everything." In fact, one of the crucial questions is whether "everything" is the universe. I believe it is not. Apart from those who answered this question based on experience to the contrary,[106] I will explain with the help of 2500-year-old Buddhist thought tradition that the one problem with "everything" is that it cannot exist, because if everything is everything, it is immediately nothing again. This fact is called in

---

[104] Fung, Yu-Lan; *A short history of Chinese philosophy*, Chapter 21, Foundation of Chinese Buddhism, N.Y., p.253.

[105] Heidegger, Martin; *Aus der Erfahrung des Denkens*, Frankf./M., 1983, p.80.

[106] Brahmananda: "Finally, the 'eye of wisdom' opens, and the infinite is perceived immediately. Ah, here is another realm, beyond the universe! The world sinks into nothing." "In samadhi the universe disappears." From: Hecker, Hellmuth; *Asiatische Mystiker*, Wien, p.107. "The universe is the illusion par excellence, the gigantic illusion, the best of all."

Indian, Pratitya-samutpada – in Chinese, Yuanqi – and is translated mostly as "dependent co-arising."

缘起

It is an unbelievably simple fact which, nevertheless, hardly anybody really considers. Unfortunately, many Asian authors also do not. The difficulty perhaps lies in the fact that Yuanqi is a mechanism or a law, rather than a "thing." A mechanism has been given a name. But with a name we imagine something fixed.

2.2 Help for the central word of Buddhist Thinking

空

Sunyata, Kong, Emptiness

2.2.1 History and etymology

The phrase "all things are empty" means that everything is nonexistent, that all experienced phenomena are empty (sunya) and vain, and thus that all objects and qualities are negated in both an ontological and ethical sense. But this negation is not mere nothingness. It rather indicates an affirmative absolute being, freed from objectifications and qualifications. The Chinese word *kong* (hollow, hole, vacant, sky) took on this deeply philosophical meaning when it was used for the Sanskrit *sunya* of Indian Buddhism.

空

In India, the term *sunya* appears quite early, in the period of Theravada Buddhism. But Mahayana Buddhism, which arose later at about the time of Christ, made this notion of Emptiness its fundamental foundation. From that time on, almost all forms of Buddhism, including those transmitted into Tibet, China, Korea, and Japan, have taken Emptiness as their most important basic idea.[107]

The Sanskrit *sunya* seems to derive from the root *svi* "to swell," the connection apparently being that something swollen on the outside is hollow inside. Indian mathematicians called the zero – which they had invented – "sunya," but *sunya* in this usage did not merely signify non-being. Likewise, while the Buddhist use of the term expresses strong negation, it has at the same time the positive connotation of ultimate reality, for it indicates immediate insight into an absolute through an affirmation that has passed through negation, a negation of relativity. Such an absolute was already recognized in the philosophy of the Upanishads in the negation expressed as *neti, neti*. This set the stage for the later Buddhist notion of Emptiness. There are discussions on the meaning of Emptiness even in early Theravadic texts such as the Pali Nikayas and Sanskrit Agamas. One of them, the Culasunnata-sutta (Lesser Discourse on Emptiness), reads:

---

[107] Nagao, Gadjin; *Madhyamika and Yogacara*, N.Y., 1991, p.209.

It is seen that when something does not exist somewhere, that place is empty with regard to the former. And yet it is to be understood that when something remains somewhere it does exist as reality.

This teaches that Emptiness signifies non-being and privation, but that at the same time an ultimate reality can be discovered within Emptiness. This passage is often quoted in later Yogacara texts as a true definition of Emptiness.

理

The character of Emptiness, as both negative and affirmative, led some Chinese thinkers to equate it with the term *Li*, 'principle' rather than with *Kong* 'empty'. This same point is stressed when it is rendered into English as "absolute" rather than "Emptiness."[108]

2.2.2 The Buddha's listing of the three most obvious confusions of Sunyata

As the Buddha explained to Kasyapa, it is not the concept of Emptiness that makes things empty; rather, they are simply empty.

> [...] Kasyapa, I say that those who refer to Emptiness as "the mental image of Emptiness" are the most lost of the lost.... Indeed, Kasyapa, it would be better to hold a philosophical view of the ultimate reality of the individual person the size of Mount Sumeru, than to be attached to this view of Emptiness as "nonbeing."

---

[108] *ibid.* p.210.

Why is that? Because, Kasyapa, Emptiness is the exhaustion of all philosophical views. I call incurable whomever holds Emptiness as a philosophical view. Kasyapa, it is as if a physician were to give medicine to a sick man, and when the medicine had cured all the original problems it remained in the stomach and was not itself expelled. What do you think, Kasyapa, would this man be cured of his disease?

No indeed, Blessed One, if the medicine cured all the original problems and yet remained in the stomach, unexpelled, the man's disease would be much worse.

The Blessed One said: Thus it is, Kasyapa, that Emptiness is the exhaustion of all philosophical views. I call incurable whoever holds Emptiness as a philosophical view.[109]

Thus, Emptiness is first of all not the image that the mind makes of Emptiness. Emptiness is, secondly, not a philosophical view at all. And Emptiness is, thirdly, also not "nonbeing."

Nevertheless, Asian thinkers publish books, such as D.T. Suzuki's *On Oriental Nothingness* and a western book on the subject called "Absolute Nothingness," which is an expression also used by many Asian thinkers. He is wrong about the "nothing" and right about the "absolute."[110]

Emptiness should, under no condition, be construed as a view (*drsti*) or a position. It has the therapeutic value of curing delusions originating from all sorts of views or po-

---

[109] Huntington, C.W. Jr; *Emptiness of Emptiness, introduction to early Indian Madyhamika*, Honolulu, 1987, p.57.

[110] For an attempt to clarify the word "absolute," see other references in the course of this text.

sitions ... it would be foolish to construe "Emptiness" as a position.[111]

and,

> According to the Sage, what is seen, heard, and so forth is neither true nor false. From a position (view) a counter-position arises, but both are meaningless.[112]

Emptiness, on the other hand, is not an assertion; an assertion always drags its negation along in tow.

> As the Madhyamika says, "I do not assert anything."[113]

> Nagarjuna: "I have no pratijna (= proposition or position) to defend."[114]

A philosophical competition with me is impossible, because I have gotten to know that "something" which can never be interpreted as a point of view.

> In his critique of all views, Nagarjuna wrote "I have no view."[115]

---

[111] Tuck, Andrew P.; *Comparative Philosophy and the philosophy of scholarship, On the western Interpretation of Nagarjuna*, Oxford, 1990, p.91.

[112] Huntington, C.W. Jr; *Emptiness of Emptiness, introduction to early Indian Madyhamika*, Honolulu, 1987, p.66.

[113] Cheng, Hsueh-li; *Nagarjuna's Twelve Gate Treatise*, Dordrecht, 1982, Introduction.

[114] *ibid.*

[115] *ibid.* p.20.

If there were such a thing as the right worldview, then that would be what I have come to know – but this cannot be 'trimmed down' to the level of worldview.

> Philosophy, for the Madhyamika, is not an explanation of things through conceptual patterns, that is the way of dogmatic speculation (*drsti*); but this does not give us the truth. The Dialectic is intended as an effective antidote for this dogmatic procedure of reason; it is the criticism of theories (Sunyata sarva-drstinam). Criticism of theories is not another theory; Sunyata of drstis is not one more drsti, but is *prajna* – their reflective awareness.[116]

and,

> *Prajna* (Skrt., literally: wisdom) is not conceptually-intellectually mediated, but directly experienced, intuitive wisdom, whose decisive moment is the understanding and the insight into Emptiness, the true-essence of the world.[117]

2.2.3 Heidegger's path from Being to Nothingness into "das Ereignis" (the 'Event')

As I have pointed out in my hermeneutic approach, I believe that what I have understood and explained makes sense. I think a "scientific" working out of subtle differences of thoughts is also valuable. However, for me it is far more fruitful to describe what has become clear to me. Whether I have understood it "correctly" is perhaps also secondary.

---

[116] Tuck, A.P.; *Comparative Philosophy and the philosophy of scholarship, On the western Interpretation of Nagarjuna*, Oxford, 1990, p.90.

[117] *Lexikon des Buddhismus*, Bern, 1993, p.174.

I was much helped by Martin Heidegger's most emphatic cry, "Beyng is not something like being." To briefly mention what has been shown to him: In the whole history of occidental philosophy, beyng as *beyng* had been lost. Only in the pre-Socratics (especially in Heraclitus) had it flashed briefly and then it had been forgotten again. To briefly outline the value of the question about being, one could say that being is not the universe, being is not the world, being is not the life, being is not the existence, being is not the *essent*.

Heidegger's essential "statement" is: Being is not something like existence (essent). Being is not existing, like the table or the angel or philosophy. Being is fundamentally of a different kind. Being is not existent, being is not there, it has no "is." The being "is" not. What should it be then? It is like nothing. Heidegger affirms this, as did Hegel,[118] and sums it up as follows:

> I have made the attempt to point out that the "being" in contrast to all "existing" is not a "being" and in this sense a "nothing."[119]

> When looking from existing to being, the being appears as nothing; the being is nothing existing, as long and as far as one may examine the being. That is, being is nowhere to be found existing. Neither does it cause existing, nor stand above existing. Being 'is' nothing. Being and nothing "are" the same. In view of the existing, being cannot be asked for, because in this realm there is only

---

[118] "So pure being and pure nothing are the same. This sentence of Hegel is correct." – "Das reine Sein und das reine Nichts ist also dasselbe. Dieser Satz Hegels besteht zurecht." (*Wissenschaft der Logik I. Buch, WW III*, p.78)

[119] Martin Heidegger in: Buchner, Hartmut (ed.); *Japan und Heidegger*, Sigmaringen, 1989, p.166.

existing and not being. From the existing, being itself becomes something existing and is not experienced as being. Philosophy, so far, is 'metaphysics'. It asks beyond the existing in the whole for an existing reason for the existing. It does not ask for being, i.e. for being *as* being. Heidegger therefore sees the necessity, contrary to all previous metaphysics, to think for the first time on being in itself. He advances into a completely new dimension of the 'question of being' which, according to his own understanding, *opens up the ontological difference in the first place. Being is nothing* existing, also not the ground of existing, also not the highest existing. "Being: Nothing: Same" (Heidegger/ Gesamtausgabe Volume 15, p.361)[120]

This epochal significance for the history of Western philosophy is highlighted below:

> The problem may lie in the fact that until now Being and Nothingness have been understood as merely opposites and can *only now* (emphasis mine) be recognized in their common, root-like unity. Heidegger's thinking has made a significant contribution to this very issue.[121]

"The root-like unity of Being and Nothingness has only now been recognized." Here, for once, two Heidegger recipients have implemented the desire for understanding with a formulation of clarity. The fundamental error of thinking – error in the literal sense – was that the Euro-Westerners did not know the Buddhist law (it really is a law). This law is called Yuanqi in Chinese and says that Being and Nothing-

---

[120] Dümpelmann, Leo and Hüntelmann, Rafael; *Sein und Struktur, eine Auseinandersetzung der Philosophien Heideggers und Rombachs,* Pfaffenweiler, p.58.

[121] *ibid.*

ness do not exist as separable single existences at all, whereas many Asian authors have also missed the Yuanqi equation.

The last generation of great European thinkers, especially Sartre and Heidegger, deal with the themes that have always been the main topics in Daoism and Buddhism. Sartre's main work is named in the title, *Being and Nothingness*.[122]

After Heidegger had recognized being as nothing, he sensed that one cannot now just set it aside and forget about the subject matter. On the contrary, this was the main "thing" at stake. He resorted to a number of stylistic devices to make this comprehensible:

> Being shows itself through its concealment. It is by being absent. Being withdraws. It is its absence.[123]

Perhaps Heidegger says it most succinctly in the following:

> It remains with the concealment of being, so indeed that this hiddenness hides itself. The absence of being is being itself *as this absence*. Being is not somewhere separated by itself and, moreover, remains still absent but, rather, the absence of being, as such, is being itself. In the absence, this veils itself with itself. This veil disappearing

---

[122] Sartre himself did not think of the Yuanqi equation, unlike many Asian thinkers where I see this as the great confusion because they could have known. With Sartre it is forgivable and highly interesting. Everything that has been thought about being and nothingness without the Yuanqi equation is tremendously exciting – but, if I see it correctly, exciting dead ends. To investigate this is my promise for the future. In this paper, I can only put forward the thesis.

[123] The whole work of Heidegger is permeated by such formulations.

into itself, as which being itself in absence means nothing but being itself.[124]

The clearest sign that Heidegger chooses to express that being has always "annihilated" or "destroyed" itself looks like this: ~~Being~~.

Being only emerges by the fact that it has crossed itself out. Being shines through absence.

The danger with these formulations is that Heidegger still speaks of "being" when it is being/nothing. In later writings he "transcends" the level of Being/Nothing and now resorts to the word which goes by the name "das Ereignis" – "the Event." However,

the Event is neither, nor does the Event exist ... [125]

The "unavailable Event" becomes the basic word.

The Event is the most inconspicuous of the inconspicuous, the simplest of the simple, the nearest of the near, and the farthest of the far, in which we mortals dwell throughout our lives.[126]

The 'Event' corresponds, in my opinion, to the main word of Buddhism – Emptiness. One of the problems with Heidegger's huge work is that he first calls the thing to be known being, but then gives the name Event to the thing to be known. If we now only state that the thing to be known

---

[124] From: Dümpelmann, Leo and Hüntelmann, Rafael; *Sein und Struktur, eine Auseinandersetzung der Philosophien Heideggers und Rombachs*, Pfaffenweiler, p.58.

[125] Heidegger, Martin; *Zur Sache des Denkens*, Tübingen, 1969, p.24 "das Ereignis ist weder, noch gibt es das Ereignis"

[126] Heidegger, Martin; *Unterwegs zur Sprache*, Pfullingen, p. 259.

is not existence (not the essent, has no "is") then the essential notion is anchored.

Basically, the same problem exists with many Buddhist authors because the thing to be recognized is called, in great confusion, alternatively nothingness and unfortunately, more rarely, emptiness.

In Daoism, too, the lack of clarity in the distinction between Dao and nothingness can often be seen. These are assertions on my part that I will flesh out more over the years.

In the end, I am convinced that the history of philosophy in East and West has been, in large part, the history of people who have been subject to certain psychological laws that have compelled them not to really confront semi-clarities and ambiguities.[127]

An obvious example is given by Hengqing Shi in his matching of the Buddhist idea of Sunyata, Emptiness, with the Taoist term *wu* (nothingness).[128]

空   Sunyata
(Emptiness)

无   Wu
(nothingness)

---

[127] It is the same laws that I addressed in the introduction. It is the form of psychology that we do not yet know that we do not know. We will have to learn that true intelligence is a sub-issue of psychological insight before the next step in (now global) philosophy can be taken.

[128] Shih, Heng-ching; *The Syncretism of Chan and Pure Land Buddhism*, N.Y., 1992, p.11.

But the confusion already begins in Daoism itself; the Dao is often not clearly distinguished from nothingness. It is the same in Buddhism, with Emptiness and nothingness.

I think it is absolutely unquestionable that Sunyata must be "translated" – I mean, understood – as Dao! And I know how strange this may sound to formalistic thinkers.

Real conceptual clarity is, unfortunately, hard to find, let alone anyone teaching it. The only thing I found in years that conveys total clarity is the following: relationality.

2.2.4 On "Relationality"

Nagarjuna understands everything in the relation of dependent co-arising and negates the 'own being' (svabhava). An "individual" is itself only in relation to the "other individuals"; there is no substantial individual.

[…] The individual components are dissolved into relationality, so that their independence is taken away from them. No "substantiality" is recognized. The pure, complete relationality is the core of Nagarjuna's teaching on dependent arising.

The "being" (bhava) is only in relation with the "nothing" (abhava); thus the being is constantly exposed to the nothing. It does not need to be added specifically that the nothingness in its turn depends on the being. […]

The affirmation and the negation are namely always in a relationship of dependence on each other so that the affirmation of a thing contains the negation of the same. The same is true in reverse. The affirmation alone and the negation alone disappear as such. […]

Emptiness carries the being/nothing and the affirmation/denial without being one of the two parts itself; to become aware of it means to become aware of the inter-dependent relationship of the parts.[129]

This could be summarized as follows:

> Being and Nothingness never occur as separate 'entities'. There is only being/nothingness as one whole: Being and Non-Being form a single piece of cloth.[130]

Being and nothingness are the inside and the outside of one and the same garment! The question is: What is the garment in its entirety? For this, it was said above – Emptiness carries the being/nothing and the affirmation/negation without being one of the two itself.

Emptiness, itself, carries the two components but it is not itself one of the two components. The "essence" or the truth of being/nothing is Emptiness. Emptiness is neither affirmation nor negation of the two components. On the basis of this paragraph, I formulated in my last main seminar work that the simplest way to make Emptiness clear would have to be: Neither being/nothing nor not being/nothing. I don't know this formulation from any other author so far and herewith I put it up for discussion.

> In the *Katyayanavavada Sutra* the Buddha, while analyzing existence and absence, has rejected both 'is' and 'is not'.[131]

---

[129] Mitsuyoshi Saigusa (Tokyo) from Henrich, D. (Ed.); *All-Einheit, Wege eines Gedankens in Ost und West*, Stuttgart, Klett-Cotta, 1985, p.109.

[130] Nagao, Gadjin; *Foundational standpoint of Madhyamika*, N.Y., 1990, p.13.

[131] Pandeya, Ram Chandra; *Nagarjuna's philosophy of No-Identity*, Delhi, 1991, p.26.

That what is, is being/nothing as a whole. But the two expressions existence and absence do not fit for this whole. So it must be called: neither being/nothing nor not being/nothing.

With "neither being/nothing nor not being/nothing," in my opinion, the thing to be said – the real thing – would be said most simply.

The traditional way to say the real (Emptiness) completely became known mainly through Nagarjuna, although it was apparently already used by the Buddha. It is called: The Tetralemma.[132]

2.2.5 The negation of the tetralemma (Catuscoti)

Now it is said: "The real is non-dual – free of any empirical statement and relatedness. It is *sunya*, devoid of any determinability. The Real is always defined in the Madhyamika treatises[133] "as transcendent to thought," as non-relative, non-determinable, dormant, *non-concludable,* non-dual. All possible determinations fall under the following four categories: Existence; Non-existence; Both existence and non-existence; Neither existence nor non-existence. The real cannot be character-

---

[132] Robinson in: Ng, Yu-Kwan; *T'ien T'ai Buddhism and early Madhyamika,* Hawaii, p.94. Candrakirti considers the tetralemma as an expedient device (upaya) that the Buddha uses in giving progressively higher instruction to the different grades of living beings. Whether, where and how the Buddha applied the Tetralemma (the Catuscoti) is probably difficult to find out, because the Buddha did not write himself.

[133] Note: In the course of this work it should become clear that the word "defined" would have to be put in quotation marks because it is, as we will see, about the eternally unknowable, the not definable.

ized by any of these propositions, singly, or in combination." [134]

The realization that, for reality, there are four possible categories – existence, non-existence, both or neither – cannot be true is at the heart of Nagarjuna's teaching. It is called the negation of the four propositions, or the negation of the four alternatives, or the negation of the catuskoti, or the negation of the tetralemma, or even the negation of the quadruple.

Interestingly enough, without having known about Nagarjuna and his Chinese successors, I "independently" came across the negation of the "four-sentence" as it was called in a seminar on Chinese Buddhism at the LMU. In the German Spiritual life there was a tireless emphasis on the importance of understanding polarity. This, amusingly, is what eventually put me on the track. Basically, Thorwald Dethlefsen taught Yuanqi (dependent co-arising) without having used this term. It was a clear thought that things exist as opposites – indeed, that they exist only as opposites. "Happiness," for example, can only exist through a contrast with happiness, for example, non-happiness. There is no happiness separate from non-happiness, both are one. So I knew that what "is" has existence only by being distinct from something. So being needs non-being to be being. I wondered, then, what is the essence of being/non-being?

And then it was clear, of course, the essence can't be one of the two halves, so being can't be the essence and nothingness can't be the essence. And somehow it was just as clear that the essence also cannot be both halves together, but also not something "outside" both halves together.

---

[134] Murti, T.R.V.; *The Central Philosophy Of Buddhism, A Study Of The Madhyamika System*, London, 1978, p.228.

And then came the highlight: By listing the four possibilities that it cannot be, it then becomes clear. There is no fifth possibility to be excluded.

绝   *Jue*
"cut off," disappear

When the four possibilities to be excluded are named, it must be complete. The whole of it <u>must</u> be fourfold. When all four possibilities have been thought out individually, each in its own right, completely rationally, and have been found not to apply, or recognized as not true, then all the work is done. What then remains is the essence of being/non-being or, better, the truth about being/non-being; what we named earlier, Emptiness.

There are several ways to "cut off" the set of four (direct translation of Chinese *jue*). The content of the four sets can be represented in the following ways. For the first type, all possibilities are enumerated as follows:

Being,
Nothing,
Being and nothingness,
Neither being nor nothingness.

These possibilities are then rejected "afterwards" as not applicable, meaning the negation of the four sentences.

In the second option, it is said thus:

Affirmation of Being,
Affirmation of nothing,
Negation of Being,
Negation of nothing.

Again, all four possibilities are rejected. Thus, Jizang can say that it is not a matter of affirmation or negation, since affirmation and negation both do not apply. So it is misleading to speak of the negation of the four propositions. This only means that the four possibilities do not apply.[135] Perhaps the literal translation is not bad at all: "the cutting off of the four sentences."

Zhiyi speaks of not meeting the four alternatives:

....affirmation, negation, synthesis and transcendence.[136]

Being/nothing is neither affirmed nor denied. It is also not the mere synthesis of being and nothingness[137] and there is no possibility to get out of being/nothingness, one cannot get out. There is no transcendence. Zhiyi says it again in a different way:

It's not self, other, both or neither.[138]
(It is not this, that, both or neither.)

---

[135] Han, T'ing-chieh; *San-lun hsüan-i chiao-shih*, Beijing 1987, p.132.

[136] Ng, Yu-Kwan; *T'ien T'ai Buddhism and early Madhyamika*, Hawaii, p.111.

[137] Hegel was the European thinker who, with the following sentence, created what was closest to what is known as a "perfect synthesis" yet doesn't quite capture it: "What is truth is neither being nor nothing, but being in nothing and nothing in Being – does not pass over – but has passed over." From v. Brück, Michael; *Einheit der Wirklichkeit*, München, 1986, p.108.

[138] Ng, Yu-Kwan, *T'ien T'ai Buddhism and early Madhyamika*, Hawaii, p.118.

Jue

"cut off"
"disappear"

The "Four-sentence"[139] is no statement, no thesis, no point of view, no theory, no assertion, no philosophical speculation and, least of all, no belief or even a religious conviction. The Four-sentence is most likely an experience, but it is also not an experience (see in the 4th chapter). The Four-sentence is the experience of the absurdity of experience;[140] the Four-sentence is transcendence in the sense that it shows that there is nothing that could be transcended.

The Four-sentence is death constantly present, signifying deathlessness.

The problem with such auxiliary propositions: First, they are not correct. Although they are optimal, they are not correct because there is no Spiritual-scientific accuracy in the humanities. Secondly, there "is" no Four-sentence and, still less, any content of the Four-sentence or even a meaning of the Four-sentence. The Four-sentence means the *negation* of the four options. The "Four-sentence" may be said because it has no content and, for that reason, can be called lack of content. The Four-sentence is the highest that can be thought. It shows the complete nullity of what we normally classify as the "world."

A common misinterpretation is that the Four-sentence is a worldview, but that is exactly what Sunyata *is not*. One cannot "praise" the Four-sentence if one has understood it, whereby understanding it in the right way means having an

---

[139] The linguistic usage "Four-sentence" is an abbreviation for: Negation of the "Four-sentence." The "Four-sentence" names the four wrong views.

[140] One might ask, what is the meaning of experience? It could be answered: The purpose of experience is to gain insights from it. It needs experience, because there must be something from which insights can be drawn.

intuitive thinking experience of it through supra-rational revelation.[141]

The "Four-sentence" is the best tool for abstract thinking with the only two dimensions that allow "exact" philosophy: everything and nothing (being and not-being).[142] The two dimensions which are (is) one, and whose essence is being explored. The "Four-sentence" thinks the unthinkable. The unthinkable is what is. What really is, everything else *seems to be*. The unthinkable is what *really* is. Our eternal problem remains that what really *"is"* is not an "is" or, perhaps more understandably, has no "is."

To say it with the voice of early Heidegger: Beyng is not existing. To say it with the voice of later Heidegger: The Event "is" not. To say it completely:

> The catuskoti exhausts the ways in which the verb "to be" may be employed in assertions: one may affirm the "is" of something, or affirm the "is not" or "both-is-and-is-not," or "neither-is-nor-is-not." In all four ways language is being used ontologically; the verb "is," in whatever variation implies the being or non-being of what the assertion is about. Nagarjuna and Candrakirti repudiate

---

[141] Whereby it is to be emphasized again and again that "suprarational" includes rational: the listing of the Catuscoti and their negation is completely rational, yes, it just exhausts reasoning completely and by doing this to the point of its demise, it is surpassed, provided that after the demise still a conscious understanding remains. "Understanding" remains the problematic word, thus: awareness. Awareness of what? Awareness of Sunyata. Awareness of Emptiness. Awareness of nonness. Awareness.

[142] The fact that being/not-being and everything/nothing are used synonymously in my work remains unquestioned here.

all of the four alternatives. They repudiate the ontological implication of the verb "to be."[143]

That which really is, is not an "is," nor is it a "not-is," nor is it "both is and is not is," and nor is it a "neither is nor is not." Anyone who seriously thinks that Nagarjuna had the pseudo-philosopher's disease of wanting to appear clever or having fun with being incomprehensible would be very wrong.

I am explaining something that is simple. So simple that you don't notice it.[144] You can't notice it either because there is nothing that it is not.

2.2.6 The most modern design for Sunyata?

A modern American thinker with no Buddhist background put the following on paper:

> Without wanting to prove it logically, I would like to give you a feeling of the reality of the "unexistence" of another universe, which enables this universe to be. The fact is that the universe which we know exists, according to the appearance, in form, space and time. The form in which it exists, except by certain scientists, is rarely questioned. The space in which it exists is taken for granted, and the aspect of time is almost never doubted. Let me ask you a few questions: What right do you have to expect that the space in which this universe exists, exists itself? Second, given the space, what right do you have to expect that the

---

[143] Mervyn Sprung in: Ng, Yu-Kwan; *T'ien T'ai Buddhism and early Madhyamika*, Hawaii, p.104.

[144] The possibility to say the "Four-sentence" shorter (Neither everything/nothing nor not everything/nothing) is a hypothesis I provide with this work.

form (matter) of the universe exists within that space? Finally, assuming the foregoing, what right do you have to expect that the universe changes, that is, that "time" passes? Clearly, we have no right to expect anything of the sort, and yet, it seems, it is all happening.

Where I would really like to get behind this is the question: What enables all this to exist in space, form and time? There has never been a universally satisfactory answer to this question. The fact that until today no suitable, universally valid answer has been developed is for me an indication that there is no answer in the usual sense that is familiar to us with regard to the formulation of answers.

Given our educational and cultural background, it is *difficult to think of a "nothing" as a "something." Nevertheless, nothing as something is the only satisfactory answer there is, since everything else falls into the realm of disagreement and controversy: the "other universe" is thus the context from which this universe came. It is that which allows this world to be by not existing in space, form and time. If it existed, it would simply be more of this universe. In a sense, this universe is the "thought" of the other universe, perhaps not even a very profound thought, although due to* the fact that we have nothing else to compare it to, we seem to think so.[145]

"Nothing" as a "something." You can't say Sunyata better. Is there a nothing that is not? No. There is only a nothing that is. One would like to think that the nothing is characterized by the fact that it is not. The nothing which is not is only the other half of being, but here we have to deal with the design of the nothing as something.

Nowhere in the history of thought does one try so hard to understand this as in the consideration and the comprehension of what the "Buddhist" term Sunyata means. Be-

---

[145] Smothermon, Ron M.D., *Drehbuch für Meisterschaft im Leben*, Bielefeld, 1987, p.201.

cause it is actually about nothing. Indeed, a special nothing, namely something that is not nothing. It is easy to forgive the extremely annoying confusion surrounding Sunyata (in almost all scriptures). It is, of course, a very difficult thought phenomenon, but in my mind there was clarity when we said: Emptiness is the context for being/nothingness. Now when Jizang[146] or Zhiyi contrast being and Emptiness, all clarity is lost for me. In my terminology, Emptiness is not to be contrasted with anything. Being and nothingness are opposite to each other, but Emptiness *has no opposite*. Emptiness is the *context for* things that are opposite to each other. Nagarjuna also speaks (analogously) of the context:

> Nagarjuna states that Sunyata is, in fact, that which allows what we perceive as existence to exist.[147]

Sunyata is the context that allows what we perceive as existence to exist. Sunyata is the framework within which the universe emerged. So the world knows an interpretation which claims to be contrary to all possible interpretations. And it is an ancient tradition which is carried on with serious effort by generations of high-profile thinkers up to the present day.

Sunyata is the direct intuition of "nothing"[148] as Sunyata. Sunyata is awareness without content. Sunyata seems to be accessible only to the type of thinker who has plumbed the phenomenon of "unconditional spiritual purposefulness" (one-pointedness of mind), and realizes that

---

[146] Han, T'ing-chieh; *San-lun hsüan-i chiao-shih*, Beijing 1987, p.133.

[147] Tuck, Andrew P.; *Comparative Philosophy and the Philosophy of scholarship, on the western interpretation of Nagarjuna*, N.Y. 1990, p.82.

[148] Strictly technical: Nothing but something.

there is nothing but the goal. And the goal is nothing: unending, and yet the final abstraction, the final detachment from *everything* concrete without anything being changed in the concrete. The concrete is seen only as what it is: Noness.

It can be called the opposite of transcendence, because nothing has to be transcended. It can also be called complete transcendence. Whoever says this is not philosophy after all has not yet understood that there is no such thing as "transcendence." There is only one old word called "transcendence" and it has no clear "identifiable meaning." One can give it meanings. One can say there is the Kantian meaning of transcendence, there is the Sartrean meaning of transcendence. Yes, but that does not mean that the Kantian or Sartrean transcendence corresponds to a reality that exists somewhere. Kantian transcendence was the bringing forth, the creation, the invention of Immanuel Kant. But it is also not that one could say the Kantian concept of transcendence is wrong. For him it was exactly right. But only for him. The Kantian transcendence concept has not been true for anybody, except for Immanuel Kant and perhaps a small fan community of unconditional admirers. Were the philosophers all free storytellers? That is what Nietzsche claimed.

With all due respect, this thesis is basically absurd. And that is completely correct, because: Consciousness always tells stories, one way or another. Subjectivity is the reality of each individual.

Nietzsche had already seen it correctly: The connection between nerve stimuli with the choice of words is almost arbitrary. The degree and limit of this arbitrariness would have to be explored. This would be valuable to be done soon. Incidentally, it would also be a fundamental approach for "interdisciplinary research" in the field of humanities.

If all philosophy and religion were only suggestions, however, this would have no influence on the only question

– of what value are they? Autosuggestion is the only form of education available to us.

No one can deny that the word transcendence has an aura, carries a vibration. And this vibration is what it is all about. The vibration that is associated with what the word transcendence wants to express is what it's all about. One can say that there is transcendence because there is a word that means that. However, this is the exact contradiction to Wittgenstein's constantly repeated thesis. Yes. We must learn to think two "opposite statements" together. Whoever said that such a thing is not philosophy was right in this sense. But it is also about the overcoming of philosophy. Only in the overcoming of philosophy will its value be truly revealed! The blossom of philosophy has not yet emerged. It is only just emerging, and then it will no longer be "philosophy" anymore. Will there be a new collective name? With Gebser's "Eteology" and Keyserling's "Criteriology" I have listed the two existing proposals that I know of.

The religious scholar Michaela Perkounigg spoke with undoubted accuracy that the "philosophy" of the future will no longer be written down by individuals, but by groups. When this future will begin, whether these groups will be international or whether the individual nations or cultural groups will send their thinkers forward, I cannot guess. In any case, I found a name in the German treasure chest that Novalis (1772-1801) had pre-written: Symphilosophy.[149]

> This is to be noted: the systematic philosophy of individual influence has come to an end. [...] Eteology takes the place of philosophy, as the latter once took the place of myths.[150]

---

[149] Novalis; *Aphorismen*, Frankf./M., 1992, p. 155.

[150] Gebser, Jean; *Gesamtausgabe Bd. 3*, Schaffhausen, 1978, p.418.

2.2.7 Sunyata in the concert of the core thoughts of this world.

From: "Philosophy Now: an inventory," Germany, 1995

The neoplatonic "One" is like the Brahman and Tao unrecognizable, unnameable and suprabeing (überseiend). Any talk about it gets caught in paradoxes as soon as it tries to express and to recognize the inexpressible and unrecognizable. In this I see also today the unsolved task of a thinking which takes up and integrates the core thoughts of the three different traditions. But it seems to be important for us Europeans and especially the Germans to get to know our own tradition first, before we are able to understand the Eastern one.[151]

What it is about (no matter by what name it bears) is unrecognizable, unnameable and suprabeing. Exactly. That is the point.

If we consider Brahman (God) as including the other theistic religions then Sunyata is significantly missing from the list. Buddhism also stands out by being missing. Its goodness lies in the fact that it does not show up on such a list. This indicates that it is excelling in its goal, because Sunyata always wants to have said that Sunyata does not "exist."

Recall from the quote above, "Any talk about it *gets caught in paradoxes.*" I would say this is the #1 feature in the current Western not-yet-understanding of this basic concept of the aperspectival world "paradox."

It is not a matter of entanglement, but rather of making things clear via paradoxes. It is true that the unrecognizable is not recognizable in the sense of a subject-object dichotomy. But it's about getting as close as possible to the un-

---

[151] Ferber, Rafael; *Philosophie jetzt: Plato*, München, 1995, p.62.

100

knowable, and this clarity succeeds through paradoxes. After that there is actually still one more trap left, but only when this entanglement dissolves does the term "paradox" come into its best possible translation – "self-cancellation." Then, and only then, do the words "God," "Dao," the "One" come to their homeopathic dissolving effectiveness.

> Because everything is Brahman (God), there is no Brahman (God).
> Because the Dao has no limit, you cannot know it.
> Because the One is All, it is Nothing.[152]

And now let's go further! It just goes on. Here you can, and must, ask further if you want the theory of everything.

> Premise 1: If the "everything" should be seen as having substance, then in order to have substance it would have to "be" and it would have to have something from which it differs in order to be definable.

> Premise 2: Then "everything" would need a "not-everything." There would have to be something outside of everything.

> Premise 3: If there is something outside of "everything," then "everything" is no longer everything.

> Conclusion: There is no "everything."

If there is "everything," it cannot set itself off from anything, because nothing would be there which does not be-

---

[152] The same, basically simple fact with all father-milk words: Something that includes everything is no longer recognizable; it can't be made out because it can't stand out from anything, so one has to admit that it doesn't "exist."

long to "everything." There is nothing outside of everything. If there was, everything would swallow that into itself.

So "everything" is always, already, welded with its other half. Everything is always already everything/nothing. That which is, is everything/nothing. This can be called irrefutably secured. But what is everything/nothing?

This is where the questions really begin. Whomever works out the unrecognizability of the unrecognizable, most clearly, *is* the only winner.

What is everything/nothing? It cannot be one half (everything) alone and it cannot be the other half (nothing) alone. After all, the truth of the whole cannot be one half. Jean Gebser addresses the right question in the following aphorism:

> Polarity is still a dualism. It is not the poles that are the determining factor, but the magnet that houses them.

- Not the north and south poles, but the earth.
- Not man and woman, but 'Man'.
- Not two focal points within an elliptical path, but the orbit as such.[153]

Not everything and nothing, but...

Everything and nothing are the two sides of the same coin. But what is the coin, as such? What is the "magnet which houses the two poles"? Only with this question will the key point be reached, and so it is necessary to ask this question. An anticipated "answer" could be: The coin is Sunyata, Emptiness. We are tempted to say that the coin is just both sides together – that is, everything and nothing at the same time. It is difficult to see that the sum of the two

---

[153] Gebser, Jean; *Gesamtausgabe Bd. 7*, Schaffhausen, p.297.

poles does not make up the "coin itself." That which accommodates the two poles is not a "whatever thing in itself." The best name so far that I have read for 'it' was in a Zen text: The "Not-anything." Actually, as we saw previously, it must be exactly pronounced as: "The not-is, not-not-is, not-simultaneously-is and not-is, not-neither-is nor not-is."

With this work, I have put up for discussion whether 'my' thesis title in its original form – "The Polarity Paradox (of everything and nothing)" – quite grasps the "thing." For the moment, the milestone is to note that we have arrived at the right question. The question is: what is capable of representing or accommodating the two opposites of everything and nothing? Can we make out the magnet, which contains the two poles, as something independent? Can we make up our own conception of something that is independent?

In the previous section "On Relationality" it was said that Emptiness supports the two legs. So we agree on the name "Emptiness" for that which houses the two poles. Unlike most writings on the subject, we have worked out a clear, unambiguous terminology. Now let us understand what "Emptiness" is.

We have already achieved a lot if we hold that Emptiness is the 'house' which shelters everything and nothing. Is there a way to explore this 'house' more deeply?

The problem, the problem of problems, the problem of all philosophy – as I will show in this work – is that it looks like there are two levels: The level of everything/nothing and the level of Emptiness. We can understand Emptiness first only by "overstepping," "ascending" above the everything/nothing. But Emptiness is the "essence" of everything/nothing.

This is what the *two truths* (see below) of Buddhism constantly point to – the everything/nothing level actually does not exist at all, because:

103

Things that derive their being and nature by mutual dependence are nothing in themselves; they are not real.[154]

The everything/nothing level is the mundane truth that we need in order to think the actual truth. I must anticipate here the two truths. The deep structure of Chinese Buddhism, Yuanqi, Erdi, they mean the same thing. They interpret Kong.

"If this exists, then that exists" is the simplest expression for Yuanqi: If everything exists, then the opposite exists automatically with it. The essence of everything and its opposite nothing, is Emptiness. And with that, the entirety of Buddhism is described: **"I have declared that which dependently co-arises to be Emptiness. There is nothing that is not dependently co-arisen. Therefore there is nothing that is not empty."** says Nagarjuna.

Pratitya-sammutpada, dependent co-arising, Yuanqi, already means Emptiness. Pratitya-sammutpada might be better translated as "existence only by mutual evocation." Everything and nothing exist only because they mutually evoke each other. But what is the truth about this "double" everything/nothing? Anyone who grasps that everything and nothing are virtually identical is, himself, almost already Emptiness because he has then already grasped that the truth cannot be one of the two poles together and also not "not both poles together."

Buddhism calls this truth Emptiness. The word of words, "Emptiness," is a "provisionary" name – temporary name.

> Nagarjuna said: It is Pratityasamutpada that we call Emptiness; it is a provisionary name.[155]

---

[154] Murti, T.R.V.; *The Central Philosophy Of Buddhism, A Study Of The Madhyamika System*, London, 1978, p.138.

And likewise: I declare whatever is of dependent origination is Emptiness.[156]

So, if we can explain "existence only through mutual evocation," then we have already explained Emptiness. "Existence only through mutual evocation" means that something comes to existence only through its opposite. Two mutual poles form an inseparable whole. The inseparability, as such, is the whole. Polarity is the *only* form in which totality can express itself. Likewise, only totality is the essence of polarity. If we say polarity, we have already said totality. The latter sentence is a translation of "Whatever is of dependent origination is Emptiness."

Dethlefsen calls polarity-to-polarity, unity. Strictly speaking, there is no polarity-to-polarity – the polarity is already the veiled unity. To name polarity in its entirety is to have already mentioned its dissolution or transcendence. Is it possible to name the primal polarity phenomenon in such a way that its own dissolution or transcendence is already represented in the name?

Gebser translates the basic concept of the aperspectival world paradox with the term "self-cancellation." When I recognize the polarity (of everything and nothing) as a paradox, their "self-cancellation" is also mentioned. The polar paradox of everything/nothing comes to an end. The end is its own transcendence, its self-cancellation. The polar paradox of everything/nothing is already Emptiness. This is my way of saying it: It is Pratityasamutpada that we call Emptiness.

---

[155] Cheng, Hsueh-li, *Empty logic: Madhyamika Buddhism from Chinese sources*, N.Y., 1984, p.88.

[156] Ng, Yu-Kwan; *T'ien T'ai Buddhism and early Madhyamika*, Hawaii, 1994, p.51.

What it all boils down to, the ultimate essence, is that there is no essence. That the whole, from which would have to be abstracted (be abstracted from), is nothing because the whole is everything and everything is always also nothing. There is only everything/nothing. Everything/nothing is already Emptiness. The final abstraction is that there is nothing left to abstract from. That, from which to abstract, has dissolved, dissipated and is actually not there. The correct interpretation is that what is to be interpreted dissolves; that nothing is there to interpret. The correct interpretation is that this interpreter, too, dissolves as well as anything to interpret. This extinguishes everything.

Sunyata is superior to the other 'strong words' – the One, Brahman (God), Dao – in that it always tries to name its non-ness first. This might be further clarified by a didactic aid:

> Sunyata-Sunyata
> Emptiness of Emptiness
> or in Chinese: Kong-Kong.

Actually, the word Sunyata in its simplest form is already the didactic aid. Here, the double naming has less emphasis than more.[157] One cannot make emphasis on something which is "inexistent."

---

[157] *ibid*, p.29. Yu-Kwan Ng emphasizes the danger that Kong-Kong could again be seen as something substantial and says that theoretically it would have to go ad infinitum, i.e. Kong-Kong-Kong.....

浴真

谛谛

Emptiness does not allow descriptors of itself. The keyword for Emptiness is featurelessness. This featurelessness, and lack of qualities, is not only free from anything but is also devoid of any desire to be free from any apparent position. The featurelessness lacks self-interest.

The problem from which we image-impaired people cannot free ourselves is that we are only able to think about contentlessness as a container within which nothing exists. But the container itself is contentlessness, is empty, and there "is" no container. The following could apply:

Sunyata is not Sunyata,
otherwise it would not be Sunyata.

If Emptiness were not empty, it would not be Emptiness. If Sunyata was Sunyata, it would not be Sunyata.

The Greek "One," the multi-denominational "God," the Chinese "Dao," the Buddhist "Sunyata," and the "Event" from the land of poets and thinkers are the main words for the unknowable.[158] The unspeakable has many names. The advantage of "Event" is its temporal novelty. It has no tradition, so and encrustation of thought-conditioning is not yet possible. Sunyata – like the other words just mentioned

---

[158] There are still many secondary words, which also want to name the epitome of the basic idea of the Spiritual, above all perhaps the "numinous." Of course, they are all only words which, as I said, find their meaning in what they point to. A word is an interpretation. A word is an interpreter of what is to be interpreted. The word is the interpretation, which interprets the thing to be interpreted. Something is and people answer by bringing forth a name. Something has been experienced and man tries to express the experienced with the help of words. Not about the other way round: The hypothesis that people have brought forth words for some reason, of which those born after say that such things do not exist, is after all only an unintelligent reaction of the belief in science that shapes today's world.

alongside it – has an enormously long tradition and it is the superior one because it emphasizes the "insubstantiality" of what is being thought. It already refers, in its name, to the misconception of being able to grasp the meaning of something. Sunyata already says with its name: You will never get me.

It could be objected that one cannot claim that the basic names of completely different directions all mean the same. But, it is precisely because they mean the same thing that the name is the interpreter.

The key to meaning lies in the word "meaning" *itself.* Meaning is what it points to. One might ask, what is the meaning of the word "meaning"? The word "meaning" has a clear meaning and that is: that the closest proximity to meaning (of a word) is in interpreting what the word is intended to mean. The content of the word can only be suggested. What is implied remains, so to speak, always in the nebulous. It always remains just an interpretation, never a determined thing. The human desire to establish something through language is completely disappointed if you just really analyze the word "meaning" once.

The meaning of a philosophical word is never clear, it is always vague. This is true for all words used by the philosopher. Except for Sunyata, because Sunyata has no meaning. Sunyata is the only word without meaning. Sunyata is the only word that does not point to anything. Sunyata is meaningless.

Emptiness is the lack of content. There is nothing in it that could be interpreted. *Emptiness does not stand for or refer to anything.*[159]

Perhaps "non-tangibility, non-perceivable" would be the translation for "Emptiness." Or "openness."[160] But we

---

[159] Cheng, Hsueh-li; *Empty logic: Madhyamika Buddhism from Chinese sources*, N.Y., 1984, p.112.

must not confuse Emptiness with the word "nothing." You can say that the word "nothing" has a meaning, but Sunyata has no meaning. While the word "nothing" is the best description for Emptiness, strictly speaking there is no nothing, because nothing is only the other half of everything. Of course, it is undeniably important that with the enumerated words – the One, Brahman (God), Dao, Event and Sunyata – very different thoughtforms will sometimes resonate. One might make a common comparison of the different thoughtforms as to their resonance. Thoughtforms – if they are on a high level – provide a powerful key to a true understanding of what is to be understood.

This is exactly today's world situation. Access to the *Philosophia perennis* (the Perennial Philosophy), to the Ageless Wisdom, was restricted in earlier times depending on geographical and 'religious-political' factors. Nowadays, any of these writings are available. Quantity can, under certain conditions, become quality – as Hegel also knew, who already tried to estimate the intellectual wealth of India in his time (but did not succeed much). Unprejudiced "Studies in cross-cultural hermeneutics"[161] have actually only existed to a certain extent since "the philosophical era I am calling it post-Wittgensteinian (which can just as easily be termed post-Heideggerian, post-modern or, simply, post-Second World War). It is characterized by the idea that it is more self-conscious than earlier periods, and by its suspicion of any and all theoretical commitments. Among philosophers of this persuasion, philosophical speculation is itself often

---

[160] And we would be back to the one who transposed the German language into beauty like no one else, the late Martin Heidegger.

[161] Tuck, Andrew P.; *Comparative Philosophy and the Philosophy of scholarship, on the western interpretation of Nagarjuna*, N.Y. 1990, p.94.

suspect and the task is to uncover or 'deconstruct' the presuppositional fallacies on which the old-age arguments and obsessions are based."[162]

2.3 The two truths

> Doctrines taught by the Buddha
> Rely wholly on the two truths.[163]

2.3.1 On the Foundation of Buddhism: The Buddha as the "Critic" of the Indian Tradition

The impossibility of expressing truth linguistically is clearer in the two truths than in any other philosophy in the world. The two truths say that there is only one, but we need a second one to approximate it for us. Yes, it is about the "One without a second." Here the Buddha doesn't want to contradict Hinduism (or other systems) at all but, to come to the One, we have to let go of the idea that the "One" can be made tangible. One of the most exciting questions of the planetary wisdom tradition was the "criticism" by the Buddha to the then existing (Hindu) tradition. This, one could say, is our oldest tradition. The original wisdom of the planet Earth postulated, for ancestral reasons, the identity of the human soul (Atman) with God (Brahman). Now came one (the Buddha) – because always again a new one must come, in order to loosen rigid thinking – who said "the Atman is non-Atman." That was it, the primordial Buddhist assertion.

---

[162] *ibid*, p.89.

[163] Newland, Guy; *The two truths in the Madhyamika of the Ge-luk-ba Order of Tibetan Buddhism*, N.Y., 1991, p.173.

And what does it mean? Yes, exactly, that is the question! Is it of any use to know this historical event? Knowledge is nothing at all. Pure factual knowledge must be classified as relatively unimportant; otherwise we will all be compelled to listen endlessly to meaningless nonsense in all of the so-called humanities. Apart from an ardent desire to understand the Buddha's intention, is there any other appropriate approach to such a matter – a matter which is one of the most significant in the true history of both philosophy and of the world?

We have lost the power of aspiration that was once ours as a child. The child is eager to understand. Adults, in their unacknowledged resignation, have stopped wanting to understand. There is no point in putting aside such a fact simply because one believes that one already has one's own correct knowledge.[164] Knowledge is nothing. What matters is to **want** to *understand*.

The biggest problem is that an understanding is only an understanding if it is comprehended at the abstract levels at which it is meant.

Common usage of language goes so far in its confusion that it even considers knowledge to be understanding. When do I know that I have understood? I hardly ever know. Anyone who has understood knows that in the next moment they will not understand again. Why is religion usually identified with "faith" by the non-experts? Those who do not understand have two options: either he believes, or he does not believe. Both are non-understanding. The word "faith" only makes sense if once there occurred a moment of profound understanding, which is no longer accessible. One then visualizes that something binding was once found, and then is able to say with surety that "at this moment I can

---

[164] As some biased so-called "religious scholars" may so conveniently do in their unacknowledged sectarian confusedness.

only remember the experience of understanding, but I stand by the fact that I have experienced it, I believe."

When is religion (or philosophy) experienced correctly? When it is experienced as THINKING. When the fine structures of thoughts are traced precisely. When the light, which lies hidden in their ways of thinking, is experienced. The light itself is intuition. "Intuition is **the conscious experience of a purely Spiritual content that occurs in the purely Spiritual.** Only through intuition can the essence of thinking be grasped."[165] Only through intuition is thought experienced as THINKING. I said we never experience thought on a purely intellectual (mental) level, but always with additionally triggered sensations. Our thinking is already a thinking-*feeling* in fractions of seconds. And this is exactly the problem. We do not think, but consider our own reactions to mental stuff as thinking.

2.3.2 Zhiyi and the Two Truths of Chinese Buddhism

Zhiyi (Chih-i), the founder of the Tientai school – who, according to my impression, is the most highly esteemed scholar among experts and participants of Chinese Buddhism – is considered to be the synthesizer of all thought structures of Chinese Buddhism existing until then. He also adopted the negation of the Catuscoti from Nagarjuna. The reference to Nagarjuna goes so far that some call Nagarjuna the founder of the Tientai school.

> The key figure in this first of the major Chinese Buddhist schools was Chih-i (538-597), who is rightly considered the greatest of all Chinese Buddhist philosophers and has been ranked with Thomas Aquinas and al-Ghazali as one

---

[165] Steiner, Rudolf; *Philosophie der Freiheit*, Dornach, 1992, p.146.

of the great systematizers of religious thought and practice in world history.[166]

A typical sentence is:

> As Chih-i writes in his commentary to the Vimalakirtinirdesa Sutra, "Reality as the two truths and threefold truth is the objective realm which is illumined through threefold contemplation."[167]

Zhiyi is especially appreciated for his fourfold teachings.[168] Many other Chinese Buddhists also loved such number games. How does this show up a millennium and a half later?

"All philosophical systems are overcome."[169] Nietzsche was the first to know, and he said it unsparingly – "There is neither Spirit, nor reason, nor thought, nor consciousness, nor soul, nor will, nor truth: all fictions that are useless."[170] Wittgenstein was the first to explain it in more detail.

This can, and must, be translated into Zhiyi Buddhist Chinese thought: There is neither threefold contemplation, nor the threefold truth, nor the fourfold teachings.

---

[166] Swanson, Paul L.; *Foundations of T'ien T'ai Philosophy, The flowering of the two truths theory in Chinese Buddhism*, Berkeley, 1989, Foreword by David W. Chappell.

[167] *ibid*, p.116.

[168] Daiichi-Shobo (ed.); *T'ien-T'ai Buddhism: An outline of the fourfold teachings*, Hawaii, 1983.

[169] Nietzsche, Friedrich; *Weisheit für Übermorgen*, München, 1994, p.196.

[170] Volkmann-Schluck, K.-H.; *Interpretationen zur Philosophie Nietzsches*, Frankf../M., 1968, p.65.

戏

论

Hsi-Lun

The threefold contemplation, the threefold truth are fictions. I hope that this was made clear enough by Wittgenstein. However, we have no choice and we have to work with these fictions. How do we work with these fictions when we see clearly that they are fictions? We work coherently when we are mindful of their fictional character. They are useless only if we are unaware of their fictional character. Fictional character should better be called model character. The threefold contemplation, the threefold truth, the fourfold teachings are models!

The great illusion is the form itself, the form of a word. The word becomes its name and is taken at face value, and then that form of thinking arises which is called by Gebser *deficient rational epoch*.

All forms are illusion but in some circumstances, as in the case we are dealing with, they can be very useful illusions. My task at the moment is to make clear that any system – however useful – never corresponds to any reality. I repeat the statement of the century from Ludwig Wittgenstein:

> A word cannot be true or false in *the* sense that it cannot coincide to reality, or the opposite.[171]

Now it can be said that the statement of the century, itself, cannot be true either. Here we may answer that after a deep understanding of the phenomenon of language – this sentence is *relatively* true because it is so important to understand.

A philosophical system is always an invention made out of the air, but that does not mean that it is worthless. On the contrary, we need philosophical inventions much more than we realize – even if they are illusionary thought ideas

---

[171] Wittgenstein, Ludwig; *Tractatus*, Frankf../M., 1993, p.97.

when seen from the highest point of view. Philosophies are language games, the most valuable thing we have.

Current Buddhism is a child of the outgoing age of reason (Gebser's terminology) and its advantage for us is that it could ignore the Aristotelian regulations due to geographical reasons, and whose overthrow means something new for us. Buddhism is also too often caught up in the rationality of the lower thinking faculties – this being, of course, a relic of the ending world epoch that can also be seen in Buddhist literature.

"Method" and "system" are the headings of the deficient philosophy of the mental-rationality Age. All systems are only models. No system can represent metaphysical reality. The systems are inventions, not reproductions, of metaphysical reality. And yet, metaphysical reality exists!

The old approach to philosophy is still caught up in this. A new philosopher comes and explains what a certain word or a certain context of words really means. In contrast to the conception of the word X of philosopher Y, I now contrast my conception of this word as correct. I have the correct definition of that word, or my context of words is the correct one. That was the old way to practice philosophy. The same is in East and West. This was not at all unexciting and is still partially valid today. But this is the old number. All systems of word strings are ultimately illusions.

The systems of Chinese Buddhism are perhaps among the most ingenious illusions that the human brain has conjured up, but its highest value will only be revealed when their illusory character, or better model character, is clear. And then the New Light will emerge from the old systems.

One could apply the concept of the language game of Wittgenstein and Nagarjuna to philosophical and religious systems – including those applied to psychology systems –

to think up light-bringing parlor games that might bring them into bloom.[172]

Wittgenstein once said that he could imagine a religion that consisted only of jokes.

The "Two Truths" is perhaps the system that holds up. Only, it is not a system because the term system implies the term "completely comprehensible through rationality." The "Two Truths" requires a comprehension that leaves reason behind, which is why it is in the heading of this section. I wrote out three of the best chapter headings[173] for the "Two Truths" from the books that were available at the State Library:

> The relationship between the two truths: Absolutely other yet striving to come together.[174]

> The two truths: not two levels of being.[175]

---

[172] From Cheng, Hsueh-li; *Empty logic: Madhyamika Buddhism from Chinese sources*, N.Y., 1984, p.119: **hsi-lun**; 1700 years before Wittgenstein, Nagarjuna used the word language game for philosophies: "In Sunyata one gives up playing the language game (hsi-lun) or conceptualization."

戏论

From Tuck, Andrew P.; *Comparative Philosophy and the philosophy of scholarship*, "On the western Interpretation of Nagarjuna," Chapter 4: Buddhism after Wittgenstein. A new game, N.Y., Oxford, 1990, p.76: "Nagarjuna was now suddenly, because of the comparisons with Wittgenstein, the most written-about Indian philosopher."

[173] See also previously in Section 2.1: What is a chapter? (What is a heading?)

[174] Nagao, Gadjin; *Foundational standpoint of Madhyamika*, N.Y., 1990, p.73.

[175] *ibid*, p.36.

The best heading is:

The Non-Duality of the Two Truths.[176]

The Non-Duality of the Two Truths, the non-two-ness of the Two Truths, the non-two of two. The two is not two. There is no two. The Two is only there to prove the One. The One can be proved only by the Two (something, in order to exist, must have a second). Truth is one; there cannot be two. For two can only be One occurring twice. But what is one? There can be no One, because it would be everything, and everything is the other half of nothing. A next heading could be: the non-twoness of the One truth, or the One-ness of the one truth. But there is none because everything already belongs to something that is One. One is therefore everything and everything is automatically nothing: One = Everything = Nothing. The Heraclitean formula about the Logos "*One* is Everything" means, if we think about it further, *One* is Everything is Nothing. The essence of these three is: One is Everything/Nothing.

One truth is no truth, there is no One.

The two truths mean that there is no truth. The result of the two truths is the one (true) truth. The result of the one true truth is that there <u>can be no one</u> (true) truth.

The end result of the two truths is: there is no truth.

That was – in my understanding – what the Buddha had to correct in the Indian tradition. There is no substantiality. The problem with the much-praised "One without a Second"[177] is: One is None. Brahman and Atman cannot "exist" either.

---

[176] Shih, Heng-ching; *The Syncretism of Chan and Pure Land Buddhism*, N.Y., 1992, p.162.

[177] Also: Non-duality, Advaita.

119

Raimon Pannikar, emeritus religious scholar, brings this to the West with his call for the de-ontologization of God and says it in one statement and without circumlocution: "God neither exists, nor does he not exist."[178] God is on another level than the one by which we understand existence and/or non-existence.

The fact that there is no truth does not mean, however, that the statement "There is no truth" is a correct statement. *Everything* that can be said is necessarily false![179]

This can be made completely clear – apart from the fact that language cannot represent facts anyway, a realization of which now only begins to dawn on mankind, with which the thinkers of the next century will have to wrestle! – through the (not yet) famous Catuscoti of Nagarjuna, which came to its sinological existence in the Sanlun school and the Tientai school of Chinese Buddhism:

There are exactly four possibilities about the statement, "There is no truth":

1. the statement is correct
2. the statement is false
3. the statement is both true and false
4. the statement is neither true nor false

All of these four possibilities do **not** apply.[180] All of these four possibilities are not true. What is true then? Nothing is true. Is it bad that nothing is true?

---

[178] Pannikar, Raimon; Das Schweigen Gottes. *Die Antwort des Buddha für unsere Zeit*, München, p.223

[179] "A word cannot be true or false in the sense that it is not, cannot, correspond to reality, or the opposite."

[180] I consider the application of the Catuskoti in every other case than the everything/nothing case to be questionable. But here it is basically

Thank God nothing is true. Everything is open. Every interpretation is possible. We are allowed to play.

The toddler's experience of the world is true – a game can be made out of every nonsense. If you watch children, you see that it actually means everything is made into a game. Every process is primarily seen as a game. In the adult world, the word "game," of course, already has another interpretation. Every word is an interpretation. However, upon closer inspection, the word "game" is a sufficient word in itself – the toddler experiences everything as the same pastime, be it eating or something else. You can clearly see how even food becomes a toy in no time.

So it could be formulated relatively adequately (most adequately) as the essence of truth is that there is not something that can be firmly established as truth. The essence of truth is *the non-existence of truth*.

"Truth is truth" can be described as the only fitting statement about truth. The fact that something concrete cannot claim the title of "truth" should have become transparent through what has been said.

Only the truth is the truth. The truth is true because it is the true thing. But what is the true thing? The true thing is the true nothingness of the truth. Only the non-ness is true.

One is only conceivable by the two, but there is no two. One and one is one because one is always one. One is beyond relationality. No relationality can be established to One, because everything already belongs to One. One is what Sartre calls the zero-reference, the unrelatedness. Another word for unrelatedness would be non-relationality. Non-relationality is the correct wording for absoluteness.

The one is actually zero.

---

the everything/nothing case, because the question is about the one truth. The one is everything/nothing. The one is the zero. But does the zero exist? This question can only be answered with the Catuskoti.

Perhaps the importance of the Sunyata concept lies primarily in recognizing one as zero.

The Sanskrit *sunya* seems to derive from the root *svi* "to swell," the connection apparently being that something swollen from the outside is hollow inside. Indian mathematicians called the zero, which they had invented, "sunya," but sunya in this usage did not merely signify non-being.[181]

What is, is the great zero and we are its zeros.

Sometimes Erdi (the two truths) is translated as "double truth." Double is the better expression, because it says a kind of "fusion" of two and their essential – to use the word "essential" to help – identity. Identity, or should I say unity? Unity or identity? Words are only tools and are, unfortunately, the only ones we have. Those who love language will have to hate that.

Also common translation terms for the two truths are relative truth and absolute truth. How do the terms relative and absolute relate?

Charles Hartshorne has contributed a key to the discussion with the following:

> In general, polar contrasts, such as abstract/concrete, universal/particular, object/subject, are symmetrical correlates <u>only as long as we think simply of the categories themselves, as concepts, and not of what they may be used to refer to or describe</u>. The moment we think of the latter, the symmetrical interdependence is replaced by a radical asymmetry.[182]

---

[181] Nagao, Gadjin; *Madhyamika and Yogacara*, N.Y., 1991, p.209.

[182] Odin, Steve; *Process Metaphysics and Hua-Yen Buddhism*, N.Y., 1982, p.132.

122

I have already tried to elucidate the 'couple' abstract/concrete by saying, "the abstract and the concrete will always bite each other." This is exactly what Hartshorne is getting at. So now another attempt of explanation on the basis of the equally (in this sense) not corresponding pair absolute/relative.

From the relative we can establish a reference to the absolute. But the Absolute Truth does not need the reference to worldly truth. From the point of view of Absolute truth, the worldly one does not exist at all. Mirror-image correspondence exists only from the relative perspective, and this is just precisely what lies in the word "relative": relatedness.

The absolute, on the other hand, is precisely the non-relative, the non-related, the absolute has swallowed the relative, so to speak. But we have no conceivable resolution of it because 'conditional arising', Yuanqi, applies, i.e. for us something, in order to be able to exist, must be distinguishable from something else. That is, related to something else. Something not related is (at least, conceivably) impossible to understand.

Is there a limit to thinking here? That we *must* immediately pull something absolute down into the relative? That, for us, the absolute is always relative? Is this the reason why Buddhism knows two truths, the worldly (relative) truth and the absolute (the actual truth, the real truth)?

This was the state of my questioning in my last main seminar paper. Today I know the answer is "Yes."

We also have the word "absoluteness" in Latin (*absolvere*, to detach) and, in Chinese, is even more drastic: *juedui*.

绝对

The word for "absoluteness" is composed of *jue* (cut off),

123

绝

and *dui* (compare):

对

Absoluteness is cutting off comparability, cutting off relativity. We cannot know the absolute. We can only know something that is related to something else; that is comparable to something else.

If I am right, what Hartshorne means by radical asymmetry points to the same thing as what I just wanted to explain by the example absolute/relative, and before by abstract/concrete. Then we could say that both Hartshornes' and my two different *word ways* point to one *idea*. I believe that Hartshorne grasped the essence of the two truths, whereby 'grasp' is already again problematic as a word. You cannot grasp it. Following makes clear that everything we know is relative, not exactly reality:

> There is not a single thing in the world which is unconditionally, absolutely real. Everything is related to, contingent upon, conditioned by something *else*. […]
>
> The long discussion of causality or Pratitya-samutpada in the Madhyamaka Sutra is only meant to show that not a single thing in the world exists in its own right, nothing has an independent reality of its own. Everything is conditioned by something (Pratitya-samutpada). The world is not Reality: it is a realm of relativity.[183]

---

[183] Singh, Jaideva; *Introduction to Madhyamika Philosophy*, Motilal Banarsidass, 1987, p.38.

绝对

Juedui

Chapter 3

On two schools of Chinese Buddhism with respective parallels to recent Western thought

In China, the Huayan school and the Chan school have had the most influence on Chinese philosophy. This was because they represented Sinified Buddhism.[184]

Tang Yijie

3.1 Transposition of the Central Theme Emptiness/Form in Li/Shi of the Huayan School of Fazang

空／色　理／事

Emptiness / Form　　　　　Li / Shi

As regarding the Theravadan, it is said that "there is no Indian counterpart of this school,"[185] which is the most Chi-

---

[184] Shinohara, Koichi + Schopen, Gregory (editors); *From Benares to Beijing, Essays on Buddhism and Chinese religion*, Oakville, 1992, p.268.

[185] Ch'en, Kenneth; *Buddhism in China, a historical survey*, Princeton, 1964, p.313.

nese form of Buddhism, and something is happening here which is probably unthinkable for the theistic religions.

理

The central word is exchanged. Kong is replaced by Li. Li is *the* word of Chinese Buddhism. Li is the most practical name of a basic word within a particular world religion.

3.1.1 On the translation of Li

I have suggested 'truth structure' for Li following Needham, who translates Li as 'organizational principle' and gives the following comment,

> Its oldest meaning is the 'pattern in things', the grain in jade or the fibers of muscles...It acquired the ordinary lexical meaning 'principle', but always retained the undertone of 'structure'....[186]

With 'truth structure' we have something quite similar to Needham's variant in the one word non-worldly (truth) and, on the other hand, the world-related (structure). Because Li wants to say *both together*.

---

[186] Needham, J.; *Science and Civilisation in China Vol.2*, London, 1956, p.558 (germ. in Capra, F.; *Der kosmische Reigen*, O.W. Barth Verlag, 1983, p.290).

Li

Li in modern Chinese means firstly fiber or grain; secondly, it means truth; thirdly, natural science and, especially, physics; and fourthly, it connotes order – each in the context of the word as it is used.

I have previously characterized Chinese Buddhism before as a synthesis of the two fundamentally different approaches to philosophy – the direct-metaphysical-related one of Buddhism, and the world-related one of the Chinese national character.

With the almost disrespectful substitution of the central word *Kong* into *Li*, Chinese thought has succeeded in translating one of the great father's-milk words in the most world-oriented way. The Chinese Buddhist Li is a word which in itself already expresses the interpenetration of the two poles – the metaphysical principle and the worldly happening.

Is there a way to translate this so that this connotation is included?

Does the Heideggerian basic word 'Event' meet the mark? There are not Events, there is only the Event. There are many occurrences but there is only one Event, whereby with the analysis of the number "one" it is already said that it cannot be about existence/absence. But now the Heideggerian Event via Japan is already translated with Chinese characters. Koichi Tsujimura writes:

> After long consideration and with great hesitation I dared to translate the Event with an old Buddhist word "jap. *shoki*; chin. *Xingqi*"

性起

> Since then, however, it remains for me a question always to be considered whether and to what extent the Shoki

can correspond to the Event or not. [...] We must also explain and discuss the Shoki very briefly: Shoki means, very roughly, the truth of "Engi".[187]

缘起

Tsujimura explains Shoki as the truth of Engi. Engi is the Japanese translation of Yuanqi.

缘起　性起

These both are opposite terms, but only one of the two counter terms is the truth. Just like "Pratityasamutpada is Emptiness." The conventional "counter term" to Yuanqi is Kong. So Xingqi definitely corresponds to Kong, which supports my claim that the Event corresponds to Emptiness.

In the four encyclopedias on Chinese Buddhism in the Munich Sinology Institute, Xingqi was included only once. It seems not to be a very common word within Buddhism. All the better it is suitable for the interpretation of 'Event'.

Event and Li, on the other hand, are additionally similar in the *way* that they were both chosen as *renewing* basic words, as new contextuals.

---

[187] Buchner, Hartmut (ed.); *Japan und Heidegger*, Sigmaringen, 1989, p.79/81.

性

起

Xingqi = The Event

However, I believe we do ourselves the greatest favor if 'Li' remains Li. This is also what Steve Odin decided to do in his book, which I see as representing the current state of planetary philosophical thought. Perhaps we can adopt Li into German. The English speaking world has already its "Li-ology."

The common translation of Li and Shi is noumenon and phenomenon. In the most overarching terminology, the priority of which I have tried to do justice to in the first place, Li corresponds to Spirit and Shi to matter. Li corresponds to 'essence', Shi to 'appearance'. Now the main formula "Li-Shi-wu-ai" is called, literally, "non-hindering of Li and Shi." Tu-shun writes:

理事无碍

"The Shi can hide Li…the result is that only the events appear, but the Li does not appear." However, "Shi is not a Shi other than the total Li. For this reason, when a Bodhisattva sees Shi, he also sees Li."[188]

There is an exact parallel here in recent Western thought:

For Heidegger, the stubborn dogma of the two spheres belongs to the inner philosophical artifice that overcomes phenomenology (since Husserl): Being and Appearance. Phenomenology, Heidegger argues, has rehabilitated phenomena, the appearing world; it has sharpened the sense of what appears. Appearance in the phenomenological sense is not an inferior, perhaps even deceptive reality behind which the actual, whether metaphysical or sci-

---

[188] Odin, Steve; *Process Metaphysics and Hua-Yen Buddhism*, N.Y., 1982, p.33.

entific, is to be sought. This "actual" is also something appearing. Phenomenology is for Heidegger not a speculation, not a mental construction, but the work of "dismantling the obscurations" and thus of "letting see uncovered."[189]

Also, concerning the numinous, it is said:

> Heidegger takes over the characteristics of the numinous understood in this way, but deletes the reference to the beyond.[190]

Here lies the Heiddegerian emphasis: If I transfer the numinous into the beyond, I forget to see it in this world. If phenomenology, according to its founder Husserl, constitutes "the secret longing of the whole of modern philosophy,"[191] then the longing is that of seeing the actual *in the appearance*. If, according to Safranski (p.104), "since Plato's time, the secret or uncanny inkling of philosophers has been that consciousness becomes a poet, and this secret kinship with poetry is not so pronounced in any philosophy as it is in phenomenology," it is not surprising that the late Heidegger pays more and more homage to poetic thinking. On the other hand, when he wanted to express something subtle, exclaimed, "One cannot simply write poetry." (Otto Pöggeler on 11/7/1994 at the Munich High School of Philosophy)…

---

[189] Safranski, Rüdiger; *Ein Meister aus Deutschland, Heidegger und seine Zeit*, München, Wien, 1994, p.106/7.

[190] *ibid* p.234.

[191] *ibid.* p.104.

理事无碍

If I think of Li as a 'design' for an incident, I can ask whether every incident has a 'design'. Does this master's thesis have a 'design' to which it more or less conforms? Is a 'design' something like an ideal? Is it I, myself, who 'throws' the 'design'? Is it an interplay between 'design' and 'throwing', with reciprocal causal connection? Heidegger prompts:

> As the thrower designs, opens up the openness, it is revealed through the opening that he himself is the one being thrown and does nothing other than to catch the counter-swing in Beyng, i.e. to move into it and thus into the Event, and only thus becomes himself, namely the preserver of the thrown design.[192]

3.1.2 Huayan and the word 'energy'

> The Hua-yen doctrine of *Li-Shi-wu-ai* is in fact a reinterpretation of the basic theme expounded in the *prajnaparamita* literature, namely, *rupam Sunyata Sunyataiva rupam* or "form is Emptiness and Emptiness is form."[193]

and,

---

[192] Heidegger, Martin; *Gesamtausgabe, 3. Abteilung: Unveröffentlichte Abhandlungen, Band 65*: Beiträge zur Philosophie (Vom Ereignis), p.304 – "Indem der Werfer entwirft, die Offenheit eröffnet, enthüllt sich durch die Eröffnung, dass er selbst der Geworfene ist und nichts leistet, als den Gegenschwung im Seyn aufzufangen, d.h. in diesen und somit in das Ereignis einzurücken und so erst er selbst, nämlich der Wahrer des geworfenen Entwurfs, zu werden."

[193] Odin, Steve; *Process Metaphysics and Hua-Yen Buddhism*, N.Y., 1982, p.24.

Einstein expresses this concept of the inseparability of material objects from their surrounding electromagnetic and gravitational fields in his work *The Evolution of Physics* when he writes: "From the relativity theory we know that matter represents vast stores of energy and that energy represents matter. We cannot, in this way, distinguish between matter and field. ... Matter is where the concentration of energy is great, field where the concentration of energy is small. ... There is no sense in regarding matter and field as two qualities different from each other. We cannot imagine a definite surface separating distinctly, field and matter."

Thus, the matter/field or object/space model emerging in recent physics is a restatement in contemporary Western scientific terms of the form/voidness or shi/li model of reality articulated by the Hua-yen school of Mahayana Buddhism in the ancient East.[194]

For many Asian scholars it is absolutely unquestionable that what is called 'energy' since Einstein is Sunyata. Professor Yeichi Yamamoto of Nihon University, Japan, writes:

The original thing which creates all things is an ultimate existence, which is not matter but not nothing. [...] The Sunyata which is the ultimate existence of all things fills the universe in the form of infinitesimal particles. Some of the particles which are condensed and fixed by the distortion of the Sunyata turn into matter. The phenomena of matter are caused by the fluidity of Sunyata which acted to matter. This Sunyata is called energy by modern scientists. The Sunyata makes everything. This is the fundamental truth of all things. This truth reveals the Buddhist teaching that mind and matter are one. This truth unites materialism with Spirituality.

---

[194] *ibid*, p.124.

Western scholars have hitherto tried to find this truth, not to rely on it, so that they have formed many perverted views. The scientists tried to find laws by establishing many hypotheses, but do not yet reach the reality of all things. They do not yet understand, for instance, what electricity really is. It will be made clear only when we see that electricity is the Sunyata which appears through the medium of metal. Electricity has no independent existence. It is a phenomenon of the Sunyata which is connected with metal.[195]

The history of philosophy in East and West is a history of 'couples'. To list some 'couples' for once:

Li - Shi
Being - Appearance
Noumenon - Phenomenon
Emptiness - Form
Actual Truth - Worldly Truth
Energy - Matter
Identity - Difference
Totality - Polarity
Absoluteness - Relativity
Unity - Duality
God - World

The populist question "Is there anything 'higher' at all?" must be accepted as a challenge by philosophy. If I affirm that 'words do not correspond to realities' then all the terms mentioned above – such as noumenon, emptiness, being, etc. – are only models. However, if I build on this knowledge and assume that the designated realities nevertheless very well exist, then they would be wordless reali-

[195] *Madhyamika Dialectic and the philosophy of Nagarjuna*, Central Institute of higher Tibetan studies, Sarnath, Varanasi, 1985, p.261/262.

ties. Can one experience wordless-realities thinking? In other words, is there thinking without language?

Krishnamurti still calls thinking a material process because the physical brain is involved and he speaks of the thought-empty awareness as energetically supreme. Immaterial energy would therefore be the most powerful. If we concretize the question "Is there anything 'higher' at all?" into "Is there anything immaterial?" we could answer – Yes, and it is energy.

> More and more, the concept that all is energy, that energy and matter are different states of one reality and can be affected by thought, is being accepted on a wide scale and is changing man's view of life.[196]

Here we have the division; a) energy/matter and b) thinking, which can influence.

3.1.3 Steve Odin's "Process Metaphysics and Hua-Yen Buddhism"

In terms of what the word "synthesis" can mean as a philosophical quality, one of the many books on Chinese Buddhism that stands out for me is Steve Odin's "Process Metaphysics and Hua-Yen Buddhism," and whose German translation particularly stands out. At this point, however, I must provide a caution. It is about the word "depth":

> If you know that God means "depths" you know much about Him.[197]

---

[196] *Share International* magazine, Amsterdam, Volume 11, September 1992, p.3.

[197] Tillich, Paul in: Odin, Steve; *Process Metaphysics and Hua-Yen Buddhism*, N.Y., 1982, p.163.

The other word for depth is intensity. Consciousness seeks it like nothing else. Our purveyors of intensity are the poets. "The words of the poet go through and through us," says Wittgenstein. If it were exclusively about depth then philosophers would really only have been poets, and not even the better ones. No, philosophy reaches a level that no poet can explore. It is precisely here that Heidegger made the decisive contribution to clarifying what thinking really is by showing the closeness of philosophy to poetry and, at the same time, the hair's breadth between them.

When intensity turns into understanding, philosophy is thrown off. Transcended intensity is awareness. Only then does consciousness begin to manage the actual. Thus, I would like to say that the works of philosophy and religion are works of utmost poetic intensity and its dimensional transcendence. What constitutes philosophy and religion is the dimensional transcendence of the "merely" poetic intensity. Philosophy and religion are, so to speak, even denser than the poetic intensity.

The poet sings: Our best moments are when the disadvantage of being born suddenly appears as an advantage.

The eteologist whispers: Recognize that which is not born and does not die as the Self.

The poet sings on the level of the pairs of opposites, the eteologist incessantly points to the level unrelated to the pairs of opposites.

Recognize that which has not come into being and does not pass away as the Self.

We find this request in every ancient Indian, and many Buddhist, scripture.[198] The dull response of the reason-

---

[198] And also with us, however, without the appeal of comprehension – Sophocles: Never to be born: Higher thinks no Spirit! *Ödipus auf Kolonos, viertes Standlied*, in Dethlefsen, Thorwald; Ödipus, München, 1990, p.107.

arrested person is that this injunction does not prod him to want to comprehend it. He conveniently dismisses it as an unproven "belief" because he does not have the intuition, the Spiritual intelligence, to experience the power of the wisdom vibration and authority of these scriptures – not to mention the fact that he is denominationally bound and non-thinking with regards to other ideology, e.g., that sort of psychology which covers up its lack of insight into the superconscious[199] by claiming to be a "man of science."

To think about something that did not come into being, you have to learn to think. This is what "Buddhism" is continuously thinking about and its executors, to this day, still quote Nagarjuna. Nagarjuna was the essential interpreter of the teachings of the historical Buddha who, himself, was only one in a countless chain of Buddhas. He said:

> Everything that comes into existence comes into existence only in dependence on something else, everything that owes its existence to dependence on something else (its "opposite") is not real. How could it? It is not from itself. The hard thing to see is that what is out of itself has no "is."[200]

It may be difficult to see but the thought is simple. This idea is called, in a new collective name, 'Martin Heidegger'.[201]

---

[199] As groundbreaking as the discovery and broad dissemination of the subconscious was, so groundbreaking will be the discovery and broad dissemination of the superconscious – which is to come.

[200] Actually: no "is" is.

[201] According to Heidegger: "Every thinker thinks only one thought." "To think is to confine yourself to a single thought that one day stands still like a star in the world's sky." *Aus der Erfahrung des Denkens*, Frankf../M., 1983, p.76.

3.2 The Chan (Zen) School and its broad impact in the 20th Century

> It seems to me that one of the most significant outcomes of Nagarjuna's teaching was the creation of Zen (Chan) Buddhism in China. During the past few decades many Westerners have been fascinated by Zen teachings and practices. But few people know that Madhyamika philosophy provides a major theoretical foundation for Zen as a "practical," "anti-intellectual," "irrational,"[202] "unconventional" and "dramatic" religious movement.[203]

"Is Chan Buddhistic?" asks Kenneth Chen correctly in his *Buddhism in China*. Is Zen Buddhism still Buddhism at all? Its declared independence from (holy) scriptures and authorities culminated in the often quoted, "If you meet Buddha, kill him." The koans have also become famous in our western countries:

> The essence of every koan is the paradox, that is, what is "beyond (Greek: *para*) thinking (Greek: *dokein*)," what transcends logical, conceptual understanding. The koan is therefore not a "riddle," since it cannot be solved with the mind; for its "solution" it requires a leap to another level of comprehension.[204]

THE CHAN SCHOOL IN CHINA
The Chinese are generally considered to be a practical, earthbound people not given to speculations about such

---

[202] Here should be "a-rational," the seminal Gebser word, if Zen is able to renew totally, otherwise it has no place in the dawning New Age.

[203] Cheng, Hsueh-li; Empty logic: *Madhyamika Buddhism from Chinese Sources*, N.Y., 1984, p.10

[204] *Lexikon des Buddhismus* Bern, 1993, p.123.

religious problems as the nature of the universe, the after-life, and so forth. When the Chinese were first brought face to face with Indian Buddhism with its rich and elaborate imagery, concepts, and modes of thinking, they were fascinated at first and finally overwhelmed and conquered. After a few centuries, however, the practical nature of the Chinese began asserting itself; it began to search for certain features within Buddhism which it could understand and practice, and in this search it soon picked on the dhyana exercise as the essence of Buddhist discipline. Dhyana, or *Chan* in Chinese, refers to the religious discipline aimed at tranquilizing the mind and getting the practitioner to devote himself to a quiet introspection into his own inner consciousness. He is made to feel an interest in things above the senses and to discover the presence of a Spiritual faculty that bridges the gap between the finite and the infinite. When he is thoroughly disciplined in dhyana, he can keep a serenity of mind and cheerfulness of disposition even amid the world of turbulent activity.[205]

We reduce philosophy (religion) to the *experience* of philosophy (religion). The practice of Buddhist philosophy is called meditation. The significant name for Zen, which is too rarely mentioned, is meditation Buddhism. The goal of meditation, however, goes far beyond contemplation. Meditation Buddhism owes its name to the Indian word Dhyana, Chinese Chan, Japanese Zen – in English, something like immersion. Immersion is a good word. What is to be immersed? Here is a place where we can briefly touch upon the psychological-philosophical sophistication of complex experiences – experiences that are literally bursting with fine distinctions. This area of knowledge for mankind had

---

[205] Chen, Kenneth; *Buddhism in China, a historical survey*; Princeton, 1964, p.350.

its first neutering by trimming it down to a collective name, namely Buddhism. In India alone, there is a wealth of different systems for the concept of 'immersion' which are worth the effort to understand. There is a wealth of psychology that rises from the depths to the heights. One can see a plateau only if one knows that it exists. The high altitude psychology of Buddhism is the science of meditation.

The overarching question might be; what is immersed and what emerges after immersing?

Arthur F. Wright, in his book *Studies in Chinese Buddhism*, compares the national spiritual character of India and China. He wrote that the "highly developed science of psychological analysis" of the Indians met the Chinese who had "no disposition to analyze the personality into its components."[206]

This encounter would become one of humankind's most fruitful achievements toward becoming spiritual. In Zen Buddhism, the already assimilated knowledge, that everyone has Buddha-nature within them,[207] finally hit the nail on the head – "I can become Buddha" became "I am already Buddha."

Potentiality became an actuality. Zen is actually all about manifesting one's own Buddha-nature and this is considered the crucial approach to everything, including even for all of our upright four-legged friends. Zen is exemplary in saying close your eyes, stop philosophizing and find the Buddha within. The practical reduction of Buddhism into the priority of the possibility for every human being to re-experience the enlightenment experience of the Buddha is called, in New American (and New German too), Zen.

---

[206] Wright, Arthur; *Studies in Chinese Buddhism*, New Haven and London, 1990, p.8.

[207] An insight that had to crystallize over centuries of Chinese Buddhism.

However, without having space to explain this in more detail now, I would like to briefly point out a misunderstanding of Zen Buddhism within the Satori concept. That is the notion that potentiality could be transformed into actuality in an instant, and then remain current forever. The true laws are more viscous.

We said earlier that in America, about 15 years ago [written about 1980], thousands of people started talking, reading and writing about Zen. A cultural critic wrote at that time, "There are two kinds of people in the world: those who have read Zen scholar Suzuki and those who have not." Today, however, there are thousands of people who actually *practice* Zen (or similar meditative/contemplative activities). And *this* is the real, the small beginning of a collective movement toward the transcendent realms.[208]

Zen is only the poster child for meditation. There are several other "Traditions of Meditation." For our subject area, there is *Traditions of Meditation in Chinese Buddhism.*[209] D.T. Suzuki on his embarrassment:

[...] That's why I am often at a loss as to how to convey the exact meaning of Chinese writers from whom translations are brought in this essay. The Chinese sentences are very loosely put together, and each compound character allows no inflection at all. As long as they are read in the original, the meaning seems to be quite clear. But if it is to be brought out in the translation, greater precision is needed to make it conform to the construction of the foreign language. For this purpose, much violence must be

---

[208] Wilber, Ken; *Halbzeit der Evolution*, Frankf./Main, 1996, p.372.

[209] Gregory, Peter; *Traditions of Meditation in Chinese Buddhism*, Honolulu, 1986.

done to the spirit of the Chinese language, and instead of translation, interpretation or paraphrase is necessary. This breaks the continuous thread of thought woven around the original Chinese characters with all their grammatical and structural peculiarities. What we might call the artistic effect of the originals is thus, inevitably, lost.[210]

Here, again, it is confirmed. The effectiveness of philosophy is strongly dependent on the strong impression of the word, which is an "artistic" one. "We should not be surprised that interpretation is not an exact science. After all, translation is not an exact science. *Science* is not an exact science."[211]

What collide here are the concepts of "science" and "art." More about this in Chapter 5 on "Implications." Now to the draft of the parallel in western thinking.

Those involved in the most immediate era of Western thought speak unanimously about the paradigm dissolution we are facing, no less a term than "the end of philosophy." Nietzsche anticipated it, while Wittgenstein and Heidegger accomplished it. Shortly before those two was another man whose self-presentation as a philosopher went relatively unnoticed to the public. He was a man of Western tradition and of the type that could withstand the future[212] – Salomo Friedlaender (1871-1946), who called himself Mynona. He resembles the Zen masters. He claimed that "any serious

---

[210] Suzuki, D.T.; *Leben aus Zen*, Frankf../M., 1973, p. 218.

[211] Tuck, Andrew P.; *Comparative Philosophy and the philosophy of scholarship,* On the western Interpretation of Nagarjuna, Oxford, 1990, p.100.

[212] On the extremely controversial and subtle topic of "self-presentation of the philosopher in public" from another point of view: see in the last paragraph "On rigor in the humanities."

book can be read humorously. Grotesque distortion is the test of the strength and endurance of mental ability, comprehensiveness and elasticity. It is a test demonstrating the accuracy of the metaphysical principle of creative detachment in observing the opposites."[213]

Two of his best definitions of philosophy may be cited as proof of his quality:

> Philosophy is the autobiography of the world.[214]

and,

> Philosophizing *means:* demanding information about the reason for the impotence of our deeply felt omnipotence.[215]

And he has the crucial theme. Goethe said, "Would not be in us God's own power, how could the God-like delight us?" Nietzsche tried but, apart from Christian mystics who are only now coming to the surface, it was a taboo in the West to experience oneself as God.[216] Already Fichte and Schelling had tried to grasp the absolute as an instance in the ego. But only Mynona brings out the real underlying core of all religions, which goes by the name of mysticism

---

[213] Cardorff, Peter; *Friedlaender (Mynona) zur Einführung,* Hamburg, 1988, p.109. "I confirm, only in the whole-body salvo of laughter philosophy finds the proof of an, at least, momentary full validity."

[214] *ibid,* p.25.

[215] *ibid,* p.89.

[216] This sad state of affairs is "due" to ecclesiasticism; this is one of the Spiritual cardinal errors of the Christian churches.

and means the experience of the Self as spiritual and divine.[217]

He adds the necessary emphasis showing a major distinction needed within Western philosophy:

> The I is "divinity in person," "*as if it were* God Himself."[218]

> "It is impossible not to be God Himself: but almost impossible never to forget this.[219]

> My embarrassment in thinking the infinite is the infinite's own embarrassment. Nothing is but the infinite. We are not only in it, we *are* it.[220]

> Faith in the Divine Self is an absolutely sure certainty of Self.[221]
> Identity philosophy is the only one that can exist.[222]

Peter Cardoff's biography of Friedlaender couldn't come up with a better quote: "Identity is that of man with God, that of man with the Infinite." I have called the question of "identity and difference" the most important one of philosophical thinking. The problem is that without difference, no identity is conceivable. But identity does not allow

---

[217] Which ultimately only finds its anchorage in the certainty of the immortality of this very "core."

[218] Cardorff, Peter; *Friedlaender (Mynona)*, Hamburg, 1988, p. 62.

[219] *ibid*, p.64.

[220] *ibid*, p.51.

[221] *ibid*, p.50.

[222] *ibid*, p.10.

difference. It is always the same problem. Whether it is called:

1. Absoluteness—Relationality
2. Identity—Difference
3. beyng—existing (terminology of early Heidegger)
4. Unity—Duality
5. God—World
6. Emptiness—Form

This means that:

1. We can only think of absoluteness with the help of relativity, but in absoluteness there is no relativity.
2. We can only think of indistinguishability as distinction, but indistinguishability knows no distinction. Our distinction of indistinguishability is already a failure of indistinguishability.
3. We can only think of beyng as something existing, but beyng is not something that exists. (terminology of the early Heidegger).
4. We can only infer unity through duality, but unity has no duality.
5. We can only approach God from the world, but whoever knows God knows that the world doesn't exist.
6. We can only imagine Emptiness as a "something" (form), but Emptiness is not a "something" (form).

And we will explain the meaning of the evolution of:

- Potentiality in actuality
- Human-nature in Buddha-nature
- Animal in Superman (Übermensch) via Human
- Man in God

We can understand them only if we think of them in context of the already quoted *idea of* Charles Hartshorne:

> In general, polar contrasts, such as abstract/concrete, universal/particular, object/subject, are symmetrical correlates **only so long as** we think simply of the categories themselves, as concepts, and not of what they may be used to refer to or describe. The moment we think of the latter, the symmetrical interdependence is replaced by a radical asymmetry.[223] (emphasis mine)

The couples are *not* couples.

Finally, we have brought the right subject matter to the forefront. Nietzsche pointed out, with his characteristic assertiveness, the uselessness of the concept of God outside of one's own Self. Mynona, finally, emphasizes the immanence of God in the Self in the same manner – for the first time since the Gnostics[224] within the history of Western philosophy as the main theme of a thinker's oeuvre. One could say that Mynona has made up for the West what Zen has done in Buddhism – the high "ideal," you are it.[225] The idea is finally grounded. You are it.

---

[223] Odin, Steve; *Process Metaphysics and Hua-Yen Buddhism*, N.Y., 1982, p.132.

[224] The contribution of the joint Sloterdijk/Macho work on gnosis, including early 'underground Christianity', cannot be overstated: "Weltrevolution der Seele" "World Revolution of the Soul."

[225] Apart from the fact that it was never in question for any student of Indian lore.

Yao

It was actually already Edmund Husserl (1859-1938), the forefather of modern Western philosophy, who provided this process with the concise statement, "harbinger".[226]

The I is not a mundane, the I is a transcendental.[227]
The "harbinger" would be what can be recognized![228]

In a perhaps still somewhat premature psychology, we will chime in, saying, Man is an adult when he has recognized the transcendental origin of his being as himself, and begins to realize it.[229]

---

[226] From *Klassiker der Philosophie, Bd.2, München, hrsg. v. Höffe, O.*; Bd.2, p.292. The term used by Husserl is "Vorzeichenänderung." There is no adequate translation of this word from the German language into English. A close translation in English might be "omen," as in receiving "advance notice" or "prior notice." Essentially, the meaning intended here is somewhat like a "pre-notification" or "initial description" of a thing.

[227] Such things can also be found in earlier epochs of Western philosophy, quite apart from Gnosticism and mysticism. But marking the crossroads highlighted here is an own path within the overall entire sea of accessible mental worlds (one could name them as the academic track of the western insight tradition, thus the philosophers who became known, or the philosophical mainstream).

[228] Something can mostly only be recognized if the information has been given beforehand that the thing to be recognized is the thing to be recognized.

[229] The "transpersonal psychology," which has so far only come to academic honors in America – and many 'underground' psychologies are already trying to follow in this today. As far as I know, the only chair for "transpersonal psychology" in Europe was held by Arnold Keyserling in Vienna.

3.2.1 The Yuanqi Law in its psychological application

One American who acknowledges Zen Buddhism as his main influence is the practical thinker Werner Erhard, to whom we owe The Hunger Project source document *The End of Starvation: Creating An Idea Whose Time Has Come* (1977). In the biography about him, by the philosophy professor William Warren Bartley, there is a passage that expresses the 'noble' aim of the world Spirit and even dares to give a "recipe for the destruction of matter by consciousness":

> The principle of re-creation, which is a variant of the Scientology principle of duplication, also needs to be examined. Werner contends that the force in *any condition in life,* if fully re-created in experience, will disappear. This is a truly cosmic principle, more abstract than the related theory of anamnesis and abreaction in Freud. This principle applies not only to headaches and minor aches and pains (processes for dealing with which are presented in the training).[230] If correct, it applies to *anything whatever*, not just to minor problems. It provides a recipe for the destruction of matter by consciousness. Such a striking general claim should most certainly be tested.[231]

---

[230] The Est training, former course in lived thinking, included the demonstration (which never did not work) of how a participant with a very severe headache got rid of it completely by re-creating the headache. The re-creation consisted of describing the headache completely, making it vivid with all possible verbalizations, e.g., paraphrasing it as the color it would have, locating it exactly in the skull, establishing its extent; would it look more like absorbent cotton or iron? etc. For further details see: Rhinehart, Luke; "Das Buch EST," München, 1983, p.70-72.

[231] Bartley, W.W.; *Biography of Werner Erhard, the Transformation of a man,* N.Y., 1978, p.263.

Bartley does this on the following pages, taking into account philosophical-historical and scientific criteria. He includes, in Erhard's biography, a good compendium of the psychology-oriented side of American thought[232] whereby its fusion with Asian thought is already further than with our European thought – although that should remain open to a final assessment.

> The 20th century possessed in the Indian-born Jiddu Krishnamurti a teacher who did not play any of the traditional language games. He rejected every tradition. He tried to get past the existing father's-milk words. Krishnamurti "preached" self-observation ceaselessly throughout his lifetime. He spoke of a state of pure attention or awareness in which the observer becomes wholly the observed. He explains this by using the example of the conscious contents of 'desire' and 'jealousy': When one observes desire, does one do it in the role of an outsider? Or does one observe how desire arises and not as if it were separate from oneself? One *is* desire. Do you recognize the difference?[233]

and,

> And then, in such observation, what is fades away. [...] In undivided attention there is no longer jealousy. Jealousy sets in only with inattention.[234]

---

[232] This, in my opinion, is its strength.

[233] Krishnamurti, Jiddu; *Das Netz der Gedanken*, Hopferau, p.54.

[234] *Leben ohne Illusionen*, Füssen, p.78/79.

Ji

The assertion is that a content of consciousness (desire, jealousy) can be observed so in such an alert manner that it disappears. With undivided attention, a content of consciousness can be observed in such a way that it disappears. What I am trying to reveal here is that the content of consciousness may occupy a small space in a momentary total state of mind – it has taken perhaps 20% of the *attention* capacity for itself – and becomes 'observable' by an 'observer' (i.e., I, the "observer," am experiencing a headache, the "observed"). If, with increasing attention, this same content of consciousness increases and prevails over other contents of consciousness, it might become 64%. At 99%, the content of my consciousness has reached its peak, and at 100% the capacity to *observe oneself* is gone because then it can't distinguish itself from anything. With full attention, I can no longer exist as a 'separate observer'. Something that is everything, is always immediately nothing. According to Krishnamurti, "If everything is jealousy, there is no jealousy. If everything is desire, there is no desire." Desire can only be desire if there is a contrast with desire and a notion of something (someone) that is doing the desiring (having an awareness that is divided between seeing an 'observer' and an 'observed').

If there is nothing but this suffering, it disappears.[235]

The metaphysical law that determines this state of affairs in Buddhist-sinological is called Yuanqi. The psychological meaning of this law is as important as the application is difficult. I cannot, of course, go into the details of application here – this would be a work in the subject of psychology. Where it comes to demonstrating the practical application of this Yuanqi, Werner Erhard was the better

---

[235] Krishnamurti, Jiddu; *Das Netz der Gedanken*, Hopferau, p.77.

Krishnamurti. He calls the process re-creation of the content of consciousness. The expression 'duplication' by Hubbard[236] still fits better – I make a double of the content of consciousness, and I re-create the content of consciousness. In other words, if I observe the headache so closely that my entire attention becomes the headache, at 100% attention the headache is recreated, duplicated, and cannot be distinguished from anything. This means it has disappeared. The copy of the headache has replaced the headache. Sunyata is the *absence* of content.

Emptiness is regarded as a medicine (yao)

药

for "curing the disease of all sentient beings." Emptiness, according to San-lun[237] masters, is mainly a soteriological device or pedagogic instrument. (chiao-ti)[238]

---

[236] L. Ron Hubbard, who drew some of his concepts from Asian philosophy, was the founder of the Church of Scientology. He was a thinker, and not even a bad one. Therein lies the problem. If a civilization is philosophically neglected, i.e. has capitulated before the higher life was Spiritually approached, then the intelligence of its successors unfortunately, almost automatically, comes into the service of the old (corrupt) way – influence for the sake of influence, power for the sake of power. Only within the overall analysis of a rotten capitalist society can the Scientology tragedy be addressed. Good thinkers with wrong values are dangerous.

[237] Sanlun is the school of Jizang.

[238] Cheng, Hsueh-li; *Nagarjuna's Twelve Gate Treatise*, Dordrecht, 1982, p.14.

教諦

Any content automatically becomes contentlessness if it is observed with undivided attention. Theoretically. It is now only a matter of formulating the law.

"All content automatically becomes contentlessness when observed with undivided attention" is a (somewhat more practical) translation of "all dharmas are empty." If you look at it closely then content is empty, content becomes contentlessness. This is the transformation of matter into spirit where the transformation *implies* a path from A to B. This is precisely the misconception. The point is that when A is 100% A, it disappears. It only *appears* that the way from A to B takes time. If A becomes completely A, this happens outside of temporality, because A is already A. The fault is that A is not fully perceived as A within semi-conscious perception (semi-attention), but only as quarter A or half A.

To make A really completely A, from a strictly technical point of view, it doesn't need more process – just more attention, your *entire* attention. The notion that it is a "non-process" also belongs to Krishnamurti. As a spiritual teacher, he demonstrated within himself a nearly permanent and unprecedented 'wakefulness'.

Werner Erhard provides a most adequate term – "transubstantiation." Matter, here, is of a psychological kind. Matter means not only physical but also emotional (psychological) matter. That 'psychological matter' is *actually* matter could not be explained except for the work of Rudolf Steiner and the tradition from which he comes. There is no room for that here. It remains to add that from this tradition (and therefore also from Steiner) mental matter is also claimed to be matter. The common colloquial term "mental matter" would therefore have to be taken literally (in the inner structure of the human being, not only as a concept of externally existing mental matter).

For us, the transubstantiation of matter into Spirit means transubstantiation of mental matter into Spirit. To be precise, first the transubstantiation of emotional matter into mental matter, and then the transubstantiation of mental matter into Spirit.

On the Term Identity (ji): Not a Synthesis in One-Dimensional Co-arising, but a Shift Beyond the Polarity of Being and Non-Being.

即

The foundational standpoint of Madhyamika is that dependent co-arising is identical with Emptiness, that this identity is the middle path of suchness. Here lie the origins of awakening, deliverance, and salvation. In China, the term *(ji)*, is used to express the identity of dependent co-arising and Emptiness as suchness.

即

In general, the word *ji* means a unity of absolute contradictory things, a synthesis of contradictory notions, like one and many, self and other. Life and death are brought together in such an identity. In Buddhism, one instant *(ksana)* does not simply denote the smallest unit of time, but is also used to signify this synthetic identity of life and death. All phenomenal beings are "destroyed from instant to instant."[239]

Everything that is experienced is immediately sent back to nothingness. Everything that is experienced is immediately annihilated. Everything that is experienced is immediately re-created, and therefore it is gone. Everything that is experienced is provided with Sunyata[240] and then it is empty, whereby it can only function because it is already empty anyway.[241]

One of humanity's most quoted sentences is *the dharmas are empty*. If the term "tradition" should contain any value then I have to hypothetically presuppose the value, and then 'play' with that until I find it out. And then it might turn out that I come to the conclusion, *the dharmas are empty*.[242] The approach I described under "Proposal of a Hermeneutic Approach" is crucial, and herein lies perhaps *the* difference between Asian and Western traditions. The Buddhists, for example, primarily try to understand, to comprehend, what is stated as true – an inside track on knowledge, which is already given, is to be pursued.

---

[239] Nagao, Gadjin; *Foundational standpoint of Madhyamika*, N.Y., 1990, p.17.

[240] Sunyata is a transparent film which when held over things brings those things to themselves, into their Emptiness.

[241] "It is not (the concept of) Emptiness that makes things empty; rather, they are simply empty." The Buddha.

[242] What is a Dharma? Among the many other uses of the word dharma, a dharma means a content of consciousness, a quantity of consciousness, a unit of consciousness, a thought-feeling conglomerate, a moment of experience, a unit of inner-temporality, a psychological presence, a moment of life, a thing, a something.

霎

那

生

灭

sha na sheng mie

On the other hand, Plato's Theory of Ideas was never understood in the West. Eventually, in the end, Nietzsche came along and dismissed Plato as an aberration. This seems to me symptomatic of the Western way.[243] Concern that an Asian reformer wants to come and overturn the whole Western tradition does not seem to be necessary there. I might venture to make an observation from the outside that Krishnamurti has already overturned it in a certain way.

Our tradition stands on even more shaky ground, the foundation of which has been destroyed by Heidegger's assertion that we have never thought what is to be thought. One could say that the Asian thinker has a basic trust in his tradition which the Western thinker does not have. Seen in this way, my approach is, on first impulse, more similar to the Asian 'truth-seeker' Xiong Shili (1885-1968):

> "That everything that comes into being instantly passes away (sha na sheng mie)" is a main Buddhist thesis adopted by Xiong.

剎那生灭

> Xiong says: "Can everything that has attained its existence remain permanently?" In this problem, I agree with the Buddhist view that everything that exists passes away instantaneously. What does instantaneous passing away mean? It means that as soon as a being comes into being,

---

[243] Perhaps this is how one might say it: The Buddhist thinkers explain what they have understood from their tradition. The European ones are lone fighters – "So that I may perceive whatever holds the world together in its inmost folds" (Goethe), so I assume that nobody has found out yet.

it immediately passes away. In other words, the moment in which it comes into being is the same moment in which it passes away. A being cannot last even a moment. [...] Such change is so small and so fast that you can hardly notice it. But if you therefore don't want to recognize this continuous sequence of the instantaneous coming into being and passing away, because it is hardly to be noticed, I will ask you: Your body is subject to a process of metabolism every moment, which you don't notice. If you do not want to deny this metabolism, why are you surprised that all things are subject to the process of instantaneous arising and passing away?[244]

---

[244] Zhang, Qingxiong; *Xiong Shilis Neue Nur-Bewusstseins-Theorie*, Bern, 1993, p. 48.

Chapter 4

Is Buddhism a Religion?

The philosopher is honest enough to acknowledge that he cannot deliver "salvation." There is a type of religious individual who wants to make "salvation" available. This is the distinguishing characteristic of a person who is later looked back upon as the founder of religion. The word redemption first occurs here. It is a word that resonates completely differently to different brains, and brings to mind different connotations (from old fashioned or outmoded to unachievable or solely aspirational). It is astonishing that all languages know this word. We can conjecture that the existence of such a word can be inferred from actual experiences of our language givers.

Now by religion we understand the goal salvation. Again, we are left with no choice but to explain one word by another. Indeed we literally define one word by another. This dilemma cannot be escaped in the whole of philology.

Buddhism, seen in this way, is indeed what the Latin German or an English speaking person calls religion. Buddhism is religion if we want to apply this Latin word to a non-Latin culture.

"Buddhism is religion" – the most banal statement is the one with the most content, if the words can be filled with content.

Of the approximately 250 wars since the Second World War, more than half were so-called religious wars. Seen in this way, 'salvation' would be salvation from religion.

It goes without saying that none of the brains involved in these wars has even come close to knowing the phenomenon of religion in its intent. Thus, the phenomenon of religion is the most misunderstood phenomenon of all, the most tragic of all phenomena.

Nonetheless, The Buddha's signpost to salvation bears the following inscription:

1. Life is suffering

2. Suffering arises from desire

3. There is liberation from suffering – through the cessation of desire, all suffering comes to extinction.

To #1: Life is suffering – There is nothing to discuss about this. This statement has nothing to do with a pessimistic view of the world but, rather, it is a representation of the facts. The more conscious we become, the more we realize how we suffer. Here is one of the few exceptions where language actually depicts the facts, without saying that life is *only* suffering.

Regarding #2: Suffering arises from desire. Anyone who has worked with this formula for many years and experimented in detail knows that it can be called "true" because the research reveals so much about it.

Regarding #3: There is liberation from suffering. Sounds like good news. Liberation lies in giving up desire.

But this is where the Buddha completely failed. He should have known that for us ordinary people it is completely impossible to give up desire. That is why there is hardly any discussion about this, because no one expects this possibility. However, as is usually the case with the Buddha, he's right. With what I called the "primal Buddhist virtue" such a thing can be achieved so that a sufficient closeness to giving up desire becomes attainable. The "primal Buddhist virtue" is non-attachment, the inner distance, non-clinging, non-sticking and in English, *detachment*.

At the point where we realize that we suffer because we desire, and that the possibility of being without desire is *de facto* impossible, we arrive to a conclusion that we need to build a very large house of understanding. This repository also has to be big enough to accommodate the probably irrefutable conclusion that man exists as the non-potentiality of not suffering in order to establish a repository of willingness to forgive.

Here is where we lay the foundation for real psychology. Here is where we are building the bridge that leads from the impossibility to the possibility of detachment. At the zenith of this bridge we recognize desire as love with the help of detachment. The *experimentum mundi* is the completion of this bridge.

But how do we get there? At what level is the analysis correct that the cause of human suffering is desire? What level of abstraction is necessary to accept this analysis as coherent? So what does desire mean here and what does suffering mean here? That would be something to experiment with. We need to think these words where they are uniquely true – on a certain level of abstraction and only there. Who can read these words on the level upon which they are given, knowing in them the direction of our evolution.

It is worth mentioning that letting go of the desire principle means much, much more than the ordinary use of what language understands as desire. It means, ultimately, giving up the attachment to life. As I said, the house of understanding we have to build will have to be big.

Schopenhauer, one of the first German thinkers to promote the importance of Buddhism, was responsible for saying "will" which must read "desire." I shall have occasion in due course to clarify this point of utmost relevance. Richard Wagner wrote about Schopenhauer – "His negation of the will to live is terribly serious, but uniquely redeeming." It must mean that the denial of the desire to live is serious, but redemptive.

In the moments in which the global desire principle is silent, only *insight* remains. The ancient name for insight is philosophia, love of wisdom.

> The following point, concerning death, *is largely beyond our understanding.* The Buddha obviously shared the belief, widespread in the early stages of human history, that death is not a necessary part of our human nature, but a sign that something has gone wrong with us. Death is our own fault. Basically, we are immortal and can overcome death and gain eternal life by religious means.[245]

"Death is our own fault."

If we take this sentence seriously, I think there are two deep reactions. Either biting sarcasm and/or the proposed hermeneutic approach – I want to understand (that). What is meant by this?

That the soul is immortal most authors will agree; between Plato and Mynona, between the historical Buddha and the coming Buddha, between Laozi and a modern Daoist, between Jesus and Drewermann (contemporary German theologist), between Patanjali and every living teacher of Indian they held this thought. Are they all crackpots?[246]

---

[245] Conze, Edward; *Eine kurze Geschichte des Buddhismus*, Frankf../Main, 1986, p.9.

[246] In other words, what do the crackpots have to tell us?

What happened in the early stages of human history? According to the preservation that bears the unfortunate collective name Hinduism,[247] and according to Buddhism, a number of Buddhas passed down the written tradition.

What about other cultural areas? Who were Yao (2357-2255 BC), Shun (2255-2205 BC) and Yü (2205-2197 BC), the legendary so-called holy rulers of Chinese antiquity?[248] Who was Hercules (8000 BC)? Who was Hermes (7000 B.C.)? When Zoroaster (Zarathustra) spoke 2600 years ago was he referring to something that already existed?

Regarding the word "eternal," the most common misunderstanding about the word is its interpretation as a sort of infinite time. But eternal does not mean temporal. Eternity is atemporality. Eternal does not mean three things: Past, Present and Future. The definition of eternity is "that which does not belong to the three tenses." He who lives out of time has eternal life. The eternal life is "now" – if "now" can be experienced as freedom from the experience of time. Really analyzed, there is no "now" because "now" is always already over again. Experimental science has discovered that "now" is, for human perception, approximately a 1/3 of a second unit. How science leads its own paradigm *ad absurdum* – the 'real' now must be some infinitely smallest measurable time unit. Only, how small we can measure? "Now" would actually be an infinitely small time. Infinity was proved by the invention of numbers – you can always add another number forward to it. It would also have to go

---

[247] To trim vast fields of distinction to a collective name always has an unfortunate effect on the general condition of mankind.

[248] "The common notion of Buddhahood is marvelously identical with that of the common concept of Yaohood and Shunhood of the Chinese Confucianism"! Albert C. Chung in: Wu, John C. H. & others; *Chinese Philosophy, Vol. 2, Buddhism; Chinese Culture Series 1-6*; China Academy, 1972, p.203.

backwards. There would have to be an infinite smallness of time. Only this could potentially be called the present. But in the end there is no present. If infinitely little amount of time is thought *ad libitum*, it is no more time. Then it is the counterpart of time, freedom from time or "eternity." These are all things that Buddhism has long thought through. Time freedom, the guiding principle of the beginning aperspectival, integral world epoch means freedom *from* the principle of time.

> Since in the "always and never" the two most extreme tenses cancel each other out in a polarizing manner (whereby both project into the time-free supratemporality), this formulation describes the essence of being as beyond any time-based structure.[249]

So spoke Jean Gebser, still the man of the hour in European intellectual history. Time freedom (freedom from domination by time) is, according to Gebser, the basic theme of the new era. Dialogues between Jiddu Krishnamurti and the physicist David Bohm were published as "The Ending of Time," and they explore the essential question of what does the ending of time" really mean concretely, psychologically? I cannot but help emphasizing again and again that philosophy and religion become real only when their thoughts come to a psychological realization. So it is hard to avoid the two paths that appeared earlier – on the one hand, the *philosophia perennis of* all times and all cultures and, on the other hand, Krishnamurti as a rejecter of tradition and initiator of a completely new beginning. Then it becomes clear: only when philosophy and religion are recognized as sub-themes of psychology, albeit

---

[249] Gebser, Jean; *Verfall und Teilhabe* (On Polarity, Duality, Identity and the Origin), Salzburg, 1974, p.80.

the most important protagonists, will we reach the height of the era in which we find ourselves. The abstract becomes concrete as psychology. Then transformation begins.

I would almost like to define the word transformation as what becomes available in Krishnamurti's psychological intelligence, for the experience of which I want to use the word "glistening." Otherwise, I know only Werner Erhard who is worth mentioning in this context for the ability to really express and 'bring to the man' transformation as the possibility and necessity of the present phase of world events. I have touched upon the similarity of the two previously in the chapter called "The Yuanqi Law in its psychological application."

Religion means salvation, salvation means overcoming death, and overcoming death means "eternal life." Everything else is just names for fear.[250] Eternal life means to experience and realize eternity in time. It means to be timeless in time. It means to control life from supratemporality and to nestle in supratemporality. The truth is that we experience time only as the present. But present, strictly thought, does not exist. So, time is eternity:

- Time and Eternity

Again we have one of these couples. But the couples are not couples. Time *is* eternity – poetically, it is always most memorable and, in the best case, also the most obvious. According to Herder:

---

[250] As long as death is not conquered, defeat awaits at the end – the attitude towards life will more or less unconsciously be one of failure.

We measure our sluggish steps according to space and time, and are – and do not know it – in the middle of eternity.[251]

That's why they say:

Doctrines taught by the Buddha
Rely wholly on the two truths
Wordly conventional truths
And truths that are ultimate.[252]

4.1 The Substrate of the Two Truths of Chinese Buddhism: Ti /Yong

体   用

Ti   Yong

Conventional truths are the method; Ultimate truths are (results) arisen from the method.[253]

Time is the method, eternity is the result. With the pair Yong (method) and Ti (result) we have one of the designations for the twofold truth (erdi), which summarizes all other pairs – the inner structure of all two-truth pairs.

---

[251] In German there is a wonderful rhyme from time to eternity (Zeit – Ewigkeit).

[252] Newland, Guy; *The two truths in the Madhyamika of the Ge-luk-ba Order of Tibetan Buddhism*, N.Y., 1991, p.173.

[253] *ibid*, p.175.

Life is the method, eternal life is the result. Samsara is the method, Nirvana is the result. BUT/AND: Samsara is nirvana.

> The Buddhas have recourse to the two truths on preaching the Dharma for sentient beings: First, the mundane truth, second the supreme truth. If a person does not know how to distinguish between the two truths, he will not know the real meaning of the profound Buddha Dharma.[254]

The couples are not couples. *This* is the message of the "double truth." The first mentioned of a couple exists only to show the result side of the couple. And only the result side is the Actual Truth.

真諦

Why, then, is the mundane side necessary at all? Because we can think about absoluteness only with one tool and that tool is relativity. Absoluteness can only be thought about through its opposite, but absoluteness *has no opposite*.

The level of the opposites is the method. The result is that the level of opposites "actually" doesn't exist.

171

4.2 Can the goal of Buddhism be experienced?

I had a moment of Sunyata within a Sinology seminar on the Sanlun School of Jizang when my classmate expressed that he could not comprehend the result of the negation of the Catuscoti. But "moment" is already saying too much, and it was less than a moment. It was like a short circuit in the brain – nothing happens – but it was ultimate. It showed that everything before has always been Sunyata; that there is nothing else. Everything that was, was also already ultimate. The ultimate is, and nothing else. It is like the dissolution of a dream, which is to see that the dream was never there, but has always been the ultimate. The dream was also the ultimate. On the other hand, I could also paraphrase the experience as the surefire revelation that everything is a dream. Wittgenstein once said: "In our waking moments, we know we are dreaming."

The Buddha is the Awakened One.[255] The Buddha has analyzed the dream.

Sunyata is a moment without time and without form, thus without an "I" and without what is called thought. It is without what is called experience, or an experience which is not experienced by anyone.

How can you describe something that is almost unnoticeable?[256]

Without a very clear hierarchy of levels of being, we will not get anywhere.

Above the concrete thinking faculty lays the abstract thinking faculty, this is for the most part already intangible. But only above the abstract thinking faculty does the level of being begin, which can be called direct perception of intuition.

---

[255] Buddha, Skrt., Pali, literally: "The Awakened One."

[256] In other respects: completely unnoticeable.

体 / 用

Ti / Yong

And this is for Sunyata, so to speak, the lowest level to which it can come. No one can explain Sunyata's revealing, but the thoughtforms that establish Sunyata are used by all authors.

As the most psychological formulation for Sunyata, I venture to say, "A highly refined, supersubtle discernment (in the sense of Gebser's perceiving and imparting)[257] as the context for intuition."

My classmate spoke as if there was a thought which he didn't understand, or a thought process that he could not accept. But this is only an indication of form-adherence to thoughts about reasoning. The "Four-sentence" has no result. Form-attachment to thoughts about reasoning things out must be let go without having the impression of losing thinking.

To realize Sunyata directly means thinking without thought – thought means form. Direct aperspectival perception is an experience of thinking without form (detachment from form), just abstraction in the last step. While my classmate still believed in not understanding the negation of the four propositions, Sunyata sat next to him and observed himself in the other as the expression of not understanding about his own being. My neighbor who declared that he did not understand (the arrow pointing to) Sunyata, was Sunyata playing hide and seek with himself.

I believe in a hierarchy of abstractions (formlessnesses). There are denser and less dense abstractions. The higher we climb, the 'thinner' the abstractions

---

[257] According to Gebser, "What we dare to speak of here takes place in the supramind. This means that for those who do not dare to exceed the limits of thought, it remains mere conjecture, while for those who perceive it is the transparency of the "ultimately real". This transparency cannot be seen, not perceived, but it can be perceived in the most effortless alertness, it can be "preserved" in the truest sense of the word." (Gebser, Jean; *Ausgewählte Texte, 1987*, p.70).

become. Sunyata would then be the thinnest of all abstractions, virtually nothing. Sunyata is like nothing, but it is not nothing. It is less than nothing. The closest possible description of Sunyata is nothingness, but it is not nothing. "It's like nothing, only better."

When Nagarjuna, Jizang, Zhiyi, and I assert that Sunyata can be thinkable, can be realized by means of the exclusion of the four propositions, this does not mean that it could be imagined or experienced.

> But the inconceivable is by no means already unthinkable, provided that thinking is not exhausted in conceiving (Martin Heidegger).[258]

Philosophical words disguise the Spiritual content. But intellectual content can only be conveyed with words. Poetic words disguise Spiritual content. However, intellectual content can only be conveyed with words. Drastic words disguise Spiritual content. But intellectual content can only be conveyed with words:[259]

> If you want to understand the sentence, you have to imagine the psychological meaning, the states of mind.[260]

Sunyata is the lightning bolt without content; the explosive device without tinder; the bomb of nothingness; the Chinese firecracker which is so quiet that it can only be

---

[258] Hempel, Hans-Peter; *Heidegger und Zen*, Frankf./Main, 1992, p.94.

[259] Heidegger, Martin; *Aus der Erfahrung des Denkens*, Frankf../M., 1983, p.33: The saying about thinking is, in contrast to the word of poetry, imageless. And where there seems to be an image, it is [...] only the emergency anchor of the daring but unsuccessful unimaginability.

[260] Wittgenstein, Ludwig; *Tractatus logico-philosophicus*, Frankf../M., 1993, p.476.

heard with the inner ear; the rocket that never goes up because it is already flying; the mail that never goes out because it is in the rocket. The perfect machine. The no-brainer, The Dao.

> Non-dual knowledge (Prajna) is <u>contentless intuition</u>. [...] The Prajna-paramita texts speak of this intuition as unfathomable, immeasurable and infinite. It is completely inexpressible, too deep for words and too all-encompassing for any distinctions. The mind, which is free from obstacles, is completely diaphanous, transparent. In this state it is not distinguished from reality and a description of this state of mind would be a description of reality. Intuition is the Absolute. In the intuition of the Absolute, there is *no consciousness of an experience.*[261] (emphasis mine)

That less-than-moment didn't change me or even make my life easier but, since it was a revelation of the whole framework, I know what this whole thing is. I know the framework within which life takes place. The framework is infinity.

The context of contexts, "Sunyata," could be called the state without.

It is about an understanding of what the planetary wisdom tradition has to offer. Sunyata is the better through-composed word for God.[262] The most real and most compact statement about "God" that I know of – taking into account the primordial relationship of relativity/absoluteness – reads as follows:

---

[261] Murti, T.R.V.; *The Central Philosophy Of Buddhism, A Study Of The Madhyamika System*, London, 1978, p.219.

[262] "Through-composed", for those unfamiliar with the term, is a form of music that utilizes a continuous progression of music without repetition. New melodies are composed for new lyrics throughout the song.

There is no reason to believe that man is alone in the universe. There is, on the contrary, every reason to believe that there exists, behind all outer appearances, an immense Consciousness to Which we give the name of God. The testimony of all the Sages and Teachers, down the ages, points to this being so.

Any other conclusion would leave out the experience of the most gifted and aware men produced by the race, which would be a foolish thing to do if one values men of the highest calibre. [...]

If I can say anything about It at all, I would say that in a sense there is no such thing as God, God does not exist. And in another sense, there is nothing else but God – only God exists.

God to me – I am speaking intellectually now, from which angle one cannot know God, but since you have asked me for a definition (you have asked for the impossible, but I shall attempt it) – God is the sum total of all the laws, and all the energies governed by these laws, which make up the whole of the manifested and unmanifested universe – everything we know and see and hear and touch and everything we do not know or hear or see or touch, everywhere, in the totality of cosmos. Every manifested phenomenon is part of God. And the space between these manifested phenomena is God. So, in a very real sense, there isn't anything else. You are God. I am God. This microphone is God. This table is God. All is God. And because all is God, there is no God. God is not someone that you can point to and say "That is God." God is everything that you have ever known or could ever know – and everything beyond your horizon of knowledge.

That God, unmanifested, uncreated, desires to know Itself in all Its possibilities, Its possible aspects, and takes incarnation – gradually involves Itself in that opposite pole of Itself which we call matter. Spirit and matter are two poles of Reality or God. Both are part of the same totality. But as they go further and further in polarity – distance from themselves – we get the pairs of opposites. We get good and evil, we get night and day, we get spirit and matter, and so on. We are trapped in the dilemma of the pairs of opposites. Through the meditation process – which takes us eventually into the knowledge of, and atonement with, the soul aspect of ourselves, the divine aspect – we can resolve these two apparent opposites. In that resolution we stand between the two. That is where the Knower stands – knowing that there is neither good nor evil, knowing that there is only One, there is only God. So you can come to know God in a certain way – but no one can talk about it.

God cannot be known from the level from which I am speaking now. It is impossible. God can, I believe, be sensed and apprehended as an experience, from moment to moment only, as That which IS when we go beyond our thought and abide in that state of unthinking awareness of the totality, without sense of self. Then we can know God. Most of us, at the stage where we are, can know It perhaps for a fraction of a second or a few moments, but that second or few moments will give one the sense of Its immortality and Its infinity. That is all one can say about that experience afterwards. You cannot describe it. As soon as you describe it you are describing a memory, you are describing an experience which is no longer God. It is something which cannot be talked about. It can only be known from moment to moment.[263]

When Martin Buber was asked why he so often used the term God, who, after all, is exalted above all earthly things, he replied:

---

[263] Creme, Benjamin; *Maitreya, Christus und die Meister der Weisheit*; Göttingen, 1986, p.118.

Yes, it is the most loaded of all human words. None has been so sullied, so shredded. That's exactly why I cannot give up on it.

The generations of men have rolled the burden of their anxious lives upon this word and pressed it to the ground. It lies in the dust and carries the burden of all of them. The generations of people with their religious parties have torn the word apart, they have killed and died for it. It bears the fingerprints of all of them and the blood of all of them.

Where would I find a word that resembles him to designate the Supreme? If I took the purest, most sparkling concept from the innermost treasury of the philosophers, I could capture in it only a non-committal thought image, but not the presence of Him whom I mean, of Him whom the generations of men have worshipped and humiliated with their tremendous lives and deaths. Certainly, they draw grimaces and write God underneath, they murder each other and say "in God's name," but when all delusion and all deception falls apart, when they face Him in the loneliest darkness and no longer say He, He, but Thou, Thou sigh, Thou cry, and when they then add 'God', is it not the real God whom they all call upon,[264] the One, the Living One, the God of the children of men?

---

[264] Here meet the two key concepts of humanity, God and Sunyata: "The origin of the common German word God is not clarified with certainty. Most likely the word is the substantivized second participle idg. ghutó-m of the verbal root ghau- '(an)rufen', according to which thus `God' would be understood as 'the being called (by magic word)'." (*Dictionary of Origin, Etymology of the German Language*, Duden 7, p. 249, Mannheim, 1.2.1989).

The etymology of Sunyata, on the other hand, is clear: the void, Emptiness, the zero, (nothingness): **God is the One invoked to lighten, nullify, make nothing, and annihilate what is. God "is" the annihilator, the emptier.**

179

I would say God is the most misunderstood of all words. The basic misunderstanding culminated in the question of whether God existed or not. The essential answer at the moment, as I have already mentioned with Raimondo Pannikar, is: Neither. In other words, God does not exist concretely, but he does exist abstractly. But the essence of abstraction is the subtraction of form. The concrete thinking faculty, which some authors profusely call the lower thinking faculty, needs form. If the abstract faculty of thought opens up something that has no form, this is non-existent from the perspective of the concrete faculty of thought. In a certain way, it is even non-existent from the abstract thinking faculty because existence or non-existence, as we commonly know it, refers only to the world of forms.

To translate the formless realms into language (that is, into form) is the problem of all wisdom. Actually, the problem arises in any attempt to pass on 'insight' which, as Sartre showed, is always an intuitive one. The creation of new words, new definitions of words or new language compositions – and the introduction of foreign words – are the first available aids. Herein displays the mark of quality to those like Gebser, Erhard and Heidegger, although Heidegger hopelessly overdid it in some places.[265] However, terminology as the transmitter of communication is the question with which the quality of being human stands or falls.

Summaries of various types

I promised at the beginning of this chapter to answer, to the best of my ability, the question "What is Chinese Bud-

---

[265] I refer here mainly to many passages in his Gesamtausgabe (Vol. 65: *Beiträge zur Philosophie (Vom Ereignis)*, Frankf../M 1989), which are not identified in more detail now, but which can also be interpreted differently.

dhism?" Always and also, in my proposals to define philosophy and religion, I have tried to do justice to this question.

When Fernando Pessoa's Faust asks whether the world exists at all, we call this poetry. When the Buddhist declares within his mental context: *the dharmas are empty, every human being possesses the Buddha-nature, the Buddha-nature is empty,* this is more than poetry. It is poetry that has been repeated so many times by so many brains over such a long time and many cultural spaces that its words have an emphasis that ordinary poetry cannot have. To experience words until they are – as someone said at the beginning – charged "with infinite meaning" would be one thing. However, the charging will only work if, as in the above example, the thought of Buddha-nature is clothed with mental matter and if sufficient thoughtforms of quality have been developed to constitute the charge. The more mental, the more effective.

To be very realistic, one has to read a lot or be able by his constitution to create and think strong thoughtforms. The quantity and the quality of the mental material with which the individual creates his thoughtforms, determine to what extent a bearer of consciousness can grasp or not one of the great phenomenon of thinking that is Buddhism. As far as what the central statement about what Sunyata means, much more capacity is required here. To experience the reality of mental matter as substantial is the preliminary stage for experiencing that mental matter that occurs completely on the abstract levels, or which constitutes the wholly abstract levels. And only when "abstract" has been pursued to the core does the eye of Sunyata's "Nothingness" smile from the plateau above for a fraction of an eternity.

Asian philosophy, in its original impulse, is essentially more oriented towards thinking about the level of being beyond reason. Therefore, more can be extracted from it for the present which has, as its theme, transcending reason. This can be somewhat represented with symbols.

[Sunyata] is constantly thinking towards the inconceivable and the "Four-sentence" is the arrow given which shows the way and points completely to it. But then there is nothing there to which it points. The arrow itself dissolves. This is, of course, only a symbol. There are only symbols for [Sunyata] and the Name [........], itself, is a symbol. The "Four-sentence" as an instrument for thinking "   ", the highest conceivable, which marks a kind of dissolution process, whose dissolution means the inconceivable.

The thinker who is attached to the concrete forms wants to grasp something with the help of his ability to think. What is at stake here cannot be grasped, it is intangible. It is the most abstract of the abstract; *the* abstract par excellence. How could the epitome of the abstract be concretely graspable?

It could be paraphrased in this way: *Sunyata (the negation of the Catuscoti) pursues the philosophical drive to want to grasp at the innermost core of things, and represents the final grip. The final grip is the one who thinks he has grasped it, and then he grasps into Emptiness. He then realizes that Emptiness is incomprehensible and can't be grasped. If, in the same moment, he sees the principle of formlessness as **the** abstract absolutum, one could then say that somebody has been seized by the Emptiness. Well, then he has caught reality for an infinitely small point of time, which basically – and this is of course crucial – is not a point of time but a point of eternity that captures reality. Then, however, he will have to recognize that the common conception of "reality" pushes forward again with its characteristic brashness.*

The interpretation of the German word *Dasein* (English = Existence) in relation to European literary history has shown that the Portuguese Faust (Fernando Pessoa's) is the one with the right question: *does the world even exist?*

The interpretation of *Dasein* in relation to European philosophy has shown that the foundation of Western metaphysics – the thesis that *something* exists, which has not been refuted by any counter-thesis – cannot be blemished. The basic question of Western metaphysics "Why is there something at all, rather than nothing?" is possibly one thesis whose inscrutability has been taken for granted due to a lack of thorough thinking. Because a true analysis could reveal that there *is* nothing. What, if thought through to the end, it was seen that there is "nothing"?[266] The openness of being could have degenerated to *Dasein* by its initial false interpretation. A different interpretation of *Dasein* could result: Everything disappears. Anyone even slightly touched by this resolution will have an idea why the Buddha has chosen the word "extinction"[267] as the image for the state to be approached.

Wittgenstein's "Philosophy should actually only be written in poetry" is rightly often quoted, and reads in full:

> I think I have summarized my position on philosophy by saying: Philosophy should actually only be written in poetry. It seems to me that this must show how far my thinking goes present, future or past. Because I have also acknowledged myself as one who can't quite do what he wants to be able to do.[268]

His colleague from the same year of birth, could. And how. One of his beautiful statements says that man...

---

[266] Strictly technical not 'nothing', but Emptiness!

[267] Nirvana, Skrt., says: "Deleting"

[268] Wittgenstein, Ludwig; *Über Gewissheit*, Frankf../M., 1994, p.483.

...can only become a shepherd of being, insofar as he remains the placeholder of nothingness.[269]

If man wants to obtain this promise by trickery and does not understand Heidegger's language, he must try to understand the essence of Buddhism. He would also get there if he understood the essence of Daoism or the essence of mysticism, but these are other language games.

The comparison of Heidegger/Buddhism is a helpful crutch to a real understanding of what both are about. The big misunderstanding, however, is that it is "thought" that there is something that is to be searched for with the concrete thinking faculty. It is with this very faculty that it cannot be found. It cannot be found with the abstract faculty of thought either. But with the abstract faculty of thought the fundamental abstractness of what is searched for can be pursued to the last consequence. And what is then found is just – seen from what we know – nothing. Something that does not relate to itself. The "non-relatedness." It is neither being nor nothingness, it is not in the external world, it is not in the internal world, it is Spiritual.

"Full religion is the great poem in loving repetition," is perhaps the best definition for religion. Interestingly, it was given by a poet and the key word here is "loving." Religion is understood by those who recognize wisdom repeated regularly as love.

Once, in all the writings I 'consumed', I found the Buddhist axiom in poetry language (it would be an interesting research if Xiong was the first to resort to poetry language, I suspect not). This is the poem that is Buddhism: A completely rational thought, which upon further thought results in the two truths and Emptiness but which, however,

---

[269] Heidegger in: Buchner, Hartmut (ed.); *Japan und Heidegger*, Sigmaringen, 1989, p.47.

184

can only be conquered, explored and affected in a supra-rational way. I quote 'not without a certain solemnity':

> All things originate from each other, without exception, in dependent co-arising. Therefore, all things, without exception, have no independent reality. In other words: all so-called things are actually empty or unreal being. Since every thing does not possess an independent reality, how could it not be empty?[270]

In Western philosophy, there is a statement which has been handed down from St. Paul: "The peace that surpasses all understanding." In German we say: "The peace that is higher than all reason."

In the more than 2000 years of the outgoing age, people have always suspected that there would be one level of being above reason. The essence of this statement is that it admits not to be able to reach this peace with reason. It is also crucial to understand that a "peace" below reason, e.g. mere pleasantness, cannot be meant here. It is about an experience, which is marked by a dimensional difference.

Due to the frequent quotation by a wide variety of thinkers throughout history, "the peace that surpasses all understanding" seems to me to be the Western statement with the strongest poetic power of all. Within this level of being – whose context is more emotional, supra-intellectual peace – one can locate and move. "The awareness of the realm of Buddhas" and the "integral-aperspectival awareness" mean this location. The movement there, which does not mean a distance from A to B, means a movement or shifting within the same state of being. This motionless movement is the intuition as the highest layer of our current

---

[270] Zhang, Qingxiong; *Xiong Shilis Neue Nur-Bewusstseins-Theorie*, Bern, 1993, p.18.

evolutionary possibilities of consciousness. When advertising the word awareness, this is the information that should be given. This is how the 'menu' for the future could read.

In simple terms, the peace that is sung about is sometimes called "the peace that exceeds understanding." Very true. This peace is like painting and music; there is nothing to understand. Understanding comes first (if required).

If I only read the book called "Der Chinesische Buddhismus (Chinese Buddhism)" and compared it to my master's thesis, you could say Daisaku Ikeda's publication is a scholarly work, precisely traces historical processes and depicts developments of thought patterns, etc.

My work, on the other hand, comes from a different impulse. I have described this impulse in me as "Proposal of a Hermeneutic Approach."

The two approaches are complementary. One is a report. Mine is an attempt to communicate the experience of being elevated through philosophy. Both are important. The former exists at the university, the latter does not. The essence of Buddhism is to understand and explain Sunyata. I said at the beginning that of the three realities of culture, history and theory, only theory is actual Buddhism. Superficial "thinking" loves to emphasize a difference between theory and practice and misses the point exactly. For, when thinking really becomes THINKING, then thinking is realization in itself, thinking is practice. If there is a gap between theory and practice, then thinking is not yet thinking. When it is true discovery, discovery is the action. Distinction alone has the power of transformation.

The assessment "Chinese Buddhist thought and Western philosophy" could be: "Long generations of Asian scribblers used, over centuries again and again, the same terminology – subsumed in language usage as Buddhism – which as its poetic and suprapoetic power now also comes into its own in the West." It can be assumed that the closing of the great book, the 2500-year work with the inscription "Philosophy of the Occident," will also soon have effects on the thinking of the East.

One result that emerged for me while writing this work was two pillars. On the one hand, the *philosophia perennis of* all times and cultures and, on the other hand, that in the same point of history in which the *philosophia perennis* becomes geographically and religion-politically available a human teacher named Krishnamurti emerges, whom "to perceive"[271] means to realize an unknown level of love, power and intelligence. And he only addresses the existing traditions with side blows.[272] He doesn't believe in anything within the *philosophia perennis.* Between these two pillars – the inexhaustible wealth of the tradition and the freshness of complete mental unconditionality – a new creativity emerged. And I can reveal it, I should reveal it. – One will (soon) come who is, in Himself, both tradition and a completely new beginning.

If one tried to wrest a father's milk word from the "teaching" of Krishnamurti, only one word will serve, it is DEATH.

Is a book 'what it says on the inside'? I raised this multi-layered question and have sought to answer it.

One book is called "Chinese Philosophy, Volume 2: Buddhism." It deals mainly with the Chan (Zen) school. The very last lines of this book are taken from the essay of the contributor mentioned in the title of the book:

> True goodness is always beautiful and cheerful, even when one is on the brink of death. I can no longer doubt

---

[271] Note: 'Perceive' here in its literal height.

[272] One could say that Heidegger takes a similar position with his assertion that the whole Western tradition has not thought the thing to be thought.

this after I have witnessed with my own eyes the death-bed scene of my dear wife, Teresa (Nov. 30, 1959). She was cheerful and thoughtful up to the very end. About two hours before her death, she whispered to our son Vincent, who was in her room together with Dr. Francis Jani, saying, "The Doctor has been standing so long that he must be greatly fatigued. Go bring a chair for him to sit down." Dr. Jani thought that she was asking for something. So he asked Vincent what her desire was. When Vincent told him what she had said, the Doctor was so moved that he went out immediately and wept. Later he told me that it was the first time in his thirty years of practice to find a dying person still so thoughtful of others. About an hour later, the Doctor called us all in for the final farewell. She was in smiles, speaking to all our children one by one and blessing them and promising to pray for them in Heaven. I was simply dazed, with wonder. Lowering my head, I prayed and offered her to Christ in the words of John the Baptist: "He who has the bride is the Bridegroom, but the friend of the Bridegroom, who stands and hears him, rejoices exceedingly at the voice of the Bridegroom. This my joy, therefore, is made full. He must increase, but I must decrease." Suddenly I heard our children call me, "Dad, mommy wants to speak to you!" No sooner had I turned my eyes to her than she leaned forward and, holding my hands in hers, said cordially, "Till our reunion in Heaven!" This lifted my Spirit to such a height that I forgot my sorrow![273]

What happened? For a few moments, the mother's milk was the father's-milk. "Mind over matter" says the Anglo-Saxon.

---

[273] Wu, John C. H. & others; *Chinese Philosophy, Vol. 2, Buddhism; Chinese Culture Series 1-6*; China Academy, 1972, p.391.

Chapter 5

Implications

5.1 The crisis of established knowledge

The crisis of *established (secure) knowledge* exists not only today[274] but I have the impression that only today it is reaching a point of decisive breakthrough.[275] Klaus Heinrich asks in his introduction to logic in the philosophy of religion, with reference to Aristotle: "What do these formulas stand against, what do they defend against, why is the opposite position not permitted? Why does a third party have to be excluded, and what would this excluded third be? Why should a contradiction be avoided, and what would happen if it were not? Why does identity have to be asserted here, and what if it couldn't be asserted? [...]"

This underlines once again, in a different way, that whatever we have come to understood so far under the principles relying on *established knowledge* is only *a small fraction, a small part of our cognitive ability, of our consciousness*. It is to this fraction – and *to this fraction science is committed* – which consequently can also open up only a fraction of the reality that exists. When we say that humans are rational animals we are actually exposing the truth that our knowledge, and especially our knowledge about man, is extremely limited and that we

---

[274] Nietzsche saw everything a hundred years before.

[275] Nietzsche: *Weisheit für Übermorgen*, 1994, p.276: "What I am telling is the history of the next two centuries."

may have to give up those "established" propositions in order to understand man. With Freud, the four basic propositions mentioned in the first paragraph broadened the scope of our cognitive abilities by introducing what he called the 'unconscious' – indeed, sometimes almost blowing it up – whereby this unconscious part comprised a much larger portion of our consciousness. From the perspective of the four basic propositions, this part still remains shrouded in darkness. Freud defined psychoanalysis as the attempt to make the unconscious conscious, such that the awareness we have of reality is expanded. Into the darkness of the unconscious he tries to bring light, since this part of us demonstrated such tremendous power.[276]

The unconscious always controlled, and still controls, the course of human affairs. Freud called rational adjustment of the unconscious "rationalization" – probably the most important term that the "humanities" has produced to date. Rationalization means linking emotion with what are *supposedly* rational statements. The undiscovered sits between true feeling and word choice with the lack of honesty with oneself due to ignorance of your own unconscious – one's original, unacknowledged emotions. Gebser's context of cultural history applies to his "philosophical" (actually eteological) point of view and is coherent there. But since we are primarily psychological (emotional) beings, it becomes clear with Freud that we have not yet arrived in the age of reason. The supposed reason is usually no reason at all. You can observe everywhere that emotional content is sold as factual, most tragically in the political sphere. Here, as in all times (except perhaps with Yao, Shun and Yü), professional lying prevails.

---

[276] Hempel, Hans-Peter; *Heidegger und Zen*, Frankf./Main, 1992, p.99.

Our species is tormented by emotions and often resorts to burning books that contain points of view foreign to our own. Now, one of the disciplines (natural sciences) which claims to be the exclusive guardian of "objectivity" has recently[277] called to burn the new and independent theories of a young natural scientist (Rupert Sheldrake) in order to protect their claims to objectivity. Our world is held in thrall by a fundamental conservatism in all areas of life, which has nothing to do with *thinking*, but with unconscious emotions. Mankind does not yet think. The true context in which language usage usually takes place is "rationalization," i.e. pseudo-reason, basically unreason. The true state of thinking in the East, West, South and North is that *we do not yet think*. We sell our emotions as "thoughts."

So the crisis of the established knowledge is, therefore, far worse than previously understood. And even worse is that *a word has no meaning that can be pinpointed*. Much of what is said or written today on any philosophical subject brings exactly the same two obscurities into the world as in the time before Wittgenstein. First, the speaker or writer believes that a statement (philosophical or everyday) which he commonly uses has the meaning he gave it in the course of his life. Then, he also believes that his listeners gave the same meaning to the commonly used phrase as he did. Surrounding both fundamentally wrong 'meanings' is a complete ignorance of the facts.

We are miles away from the cautiousness that would arise if we had integrated Wittgenstein (or Buddhism). Such cautiousness can only be achieved by someone who is not afraid of the permanent admission of his own not-knowing and inability in the face of the subjection with which living and dying have always preceded us. All that academic philosophical fuss is based on very simple psychological pat-

---

[277] Via TV Science Magazine in England.

terns and as long as it is not known that the first feature of strength is the ability to admit weakness, will the LIGHT still not be understood by the world. Within darkness, darkness does not stand out as darkness. But what is really tragic is that the old phrase continues to hold true: The Light came into the darkness, but the darkness did not understand it.

Wang Tchin (1725-1792), catalogued by Forke as a Confucian Buddhist, said this as early as the 18th century:

> The reader thinks and feels differently than the writer. He remains lonely with his sensations and thoughts, because these are taken up and reshaped in the mind of the listener according to their own nature.[278]

This applies to every conversation. "Lonely" is the key word here. We are the beings who do everything possible to avoid confronting this fundamental loneliness. The quality of our previous philosophy corresponds exactly to our low level awareness of this loneliness.

In less than a minute of speaking time within any "philosophical" conversation, these three misconceptions occur:

1. misconception: a word has a definition
2. misconception: a word has a binding definition
3. misconception: my definition of the word is the binding definition of the word

This phenomenon also appears similarly in music. Composer Mathias Spahlinger characterizes one of the crucial differences between traditional and New Music in re-

---

[278] Forke, Alfred; *Geschichte der neueren chinesischen Philosophie*, Hamburg, 1964, p.560.

sponse to the question of what insight lies behind New Music:

> If one wanted to make a doctrine out of it, it would be called: "Everything that is, is what it is, only in and through its context." And this fact was ignored in traditional music, necessarily hidden, one still "believed" in "clear" identifications (scale, harmonics). One was just not aware that "everything that is, what it is, is only in and through its context." The crucial difference to traditional music is that in New Music this absolute relativism is continuously discussed.[279]

There is nothing absolute except absolute relativism. Only the relative is absolute. It is not true, but you have to say it because it is true. And it really is true. Another way to translate "Whatever is of dependent origination is Emptiness" is to say: *That which is, is what it is, only because of relativity. To think all the way through the phenomenon of "relativity" as relationality means revealing absoluteness.*

The most successful philosophical theory of all times is called "relativity theory." Much older is the absoluteness theory.

Wherever I look the old philosophy, for the most part, is still being practiced,[280] i.e. philosophy that is not yet aware that nothing remains of it when it is shown that it only applies if false identifications are believed.[281]

---

[279] Radiobroadcast Bayerischer Rundfunk 2: composer portrait; private recording.

[280] Exactly according to how traditional classical music is still played everywhere, although the New Music can show more than a 100 years.

[281] The bogus identification is that a word is by itself what it is. Of course "freedom" is "freedom," but no two people will understand the same under "freedom." "Freedom" is therefore just not "freedom"!

Some composers of New Music (NM) are among the really interesting "philosophers" of these days, and it is here that the tragedy becomes clear.

There is no more philosophy, just as there is no more classical music (except, of course, as phenomena of the past). So, I have been compelled during this whole work to continue using the old word because there is not yet consensus about a more advanced one!

In some respects, a new parameter might have spelled out parameters regarding how something to say might be presented:

Anything that is well said, is a word of the Buddha.[282]

Agreed, but only if the operator of the word knows that he does not know. It more likely remains, however, that the poorly said, the hesitant, the self-relativizing, the loneliness-conscious, the cautious is the word of the Buddha.[283]

---

[282] Adhyasayasamchodana Sutra, in: Kennedy, Alex; *Buddhism for today*, Glasgow, 1988, p.8.

[283] "Don't think of timid assertion as assertion of timidity." Ludwig Wittgenstein, *Tractatus*, p.517.

5.1.1 New topics

道

The eternal Dao dwells in all, in murderers and harlots as
well as in philosophers and poets. They all carry the inde-
structible treasure within them, and not one is better than
another.[284]

I mentioned the primary importance of Jean Gebser in
recent European thought and his affinity for Asia. His
recognition of the quality and primacy of Asian themes is
particularly evident and almost testamentary in the subtitle
of his last work *On Polarity, Duality, Identity and the
Origin*[285]. These are exactly the concepts that should be
thought about.[286]

---

[284] Borel, Henri in: Dethlefsen, Thorwald; *Gut und Böse*, München,
1989, S.33.

[285] Gebser, Jean; *Verfall und Teilhabe* (On Polarity, Duality, Identity and
the Origin), Salzburg, 1974.

[286] Polarity, duality and identity were what all my work was about, but
what should be the origin? I don't know, I really don't know. Is there
somewhere something that 'says on it' "origin" and then "origin" is also
'in it'? With Wittgenstein we have denied this. But the word "origin"
wants to say something. One would like to think that the word "origin"
(German: Ursprung), wants to express something quite weighty. But
what?

Dao

The theme that was missing in the West is that opposites produce each other, bring each other out. Something is always inextricably linked to something from which it differs. Light, for example, owes its existence to darkness; darkness owes its existence to light. Strictly speaking, there is only "light/darkness." Once the one pole emerges, the other one must also appear. Opposites are actually an inseparable **whole**. The expressions polarity and duality give account to this phenomenon. Things exist as 'pairs' – Light/Dark, real/unreal, yin/yang, birth/death, happiness/unhappiness, form/Emptiness, man/woman, and the couplet of being/non-being. Or everything/nothing.

The Zen master Huineng makes out thirty-six such "pairs of opposites."[287] Already the Yijing (I Ching)[288] has, according to Xiong, "opposites produce each other" as its main principle. In any case, Laozi lines up mutually dependent opposites in a poetic manner, saying:

> All these pairs of opposites belong to the realm of relativity and the Sage does not dwell on them, but rises above them.[289]

The problem of dualities presents an impenetrable problem for Aristotelian logic. The two truths are the "solution" for the pairs of opposites. I had hoped to get closer to this "solution" in this work, but I rarely succeeded. This "solution" is too complex and difficult to express within the

[287] Wu, John C. H. & others; *Chinese Philosophy, Vol. 2, Buddhism; Chinese Culture Series 1-6*; China Academy, 1972, p.13.

[288] Zhang, Qingxiong; *Xiong Shilis Neue Nur-Bewusstseins-Theorie*, Bern, 1993, p.41/42.

[289] Wu, John C. H. & others; *Chinese Philosophy, Vol. 2, Buddhism; Chinese Culture Series 1-6*; China Academy, 1972, p.12.

context of this work, which had to be devoted to certain indispensable foundation creations. I am happy to have at least touched upon it.

In this master thesis I can only afford to clarify the priorities of topics, ambiguities in the previous terminology and certain other aspects. The rest must remain a promise for the future.

We could contrast the terms polarity and duality as follows: Duality is the view of two opposing forces, each existing separately. Defined in this way, duality would be a false view. The followers of polarity claim that the two forces cannot exist separately, but are dependent on each other. Both forces are seen as part of the same coin and owe their existence to the other half. This corresponds to the Eastern teaching known as 'dependent co-arising' (Skt.: Pratityasamutpada; Chi.: Yuanqi). Thus, dualism would dissolve in the understanding of polarity. But polarity would still remain the form in which totality can express itself.

> Today dualism has fulfilled its historical task, which was to give to the Western notion of spirit that tension, that sense of direction, thanks to which it became possible for it to dissolve it after unspeakable toil and suffering, that is, to find a new level, a further relationship.[290]

and,

> If it is possible to clearly resolve the opposite pair of space and time, to prove that both do not exist and to show that they are just one and the same (which I do not want to call Rilke's "world inner space," because this opens up a new counter-term "world outer space"), then it will be easy to prove that pairs of terms like Soul and Body; Heaven and Earth; Masculine and Feminine are al-

---

[290] Gebser, Jean; *Gesamtausgabe Bd.7*, Schaffhausen, p.275.

so only misconceptions that arise from man's *temporary* inability to describe a thing or person. A concept can only be thought of and realized comprehensively if it is artificially represented by a so-called opposite. (remember the Chinese approach: "measure" equals "short-long"). Why has it never been consistently and correctly to think through to the end: "les extremes se touchent (the extremes touch each other)"?[291]

One could answer: Because Aristotle forbade it. But it turns out that he will have only forbid it for 2300 years to half of mankind. "Opposites exclude each other" we were told. The whole truth is that opposites condition each other. Only by opposition, A is A. A needs something that is not-A, to be A. Otherwise, it cannot be A.

> Opposites are a tool for making thoughts comprehensible. Opposites provide measure and value. The unconscious does not know them. The consciousness shapes them. But what is important is to go beyond them. So, for example, B to stand above good and evil but not "beyond good and evil," which is, first of all, just one thing. Secondly, what is offside is that it still allows for a "this side." But standing above good and evil is misleading because it contains, at the same time: between good and evil. Standing above good and evil is to stand in the whole of reality.[292]

So, one cannot formulate it adequately, but "above" already says it. Also Laozi (Lao-tse) cannot express it differently than "above."

> If a person lives in a culture where the correctness of Aristotelian logic is not doubted, it is exceedingly difficult,

---

[291] *ibid*, p.276.

[292] *ibid*, p.275.

199

if not impossible, for him to become aware of such feelings that contradict Aristotelian logic and are therefore nonsensical from the point of view of his culture. A good example is Freud's concept of ambivalence, which states that one can feel love and hate for the same person at the same time. This feeling, quite "logical" from the point of view of paradoxical logic, is nonsensical from that of Aristotelian logic. The result is that most people find it exceedingly difficult to become aware of ambivalent feelings. If they are aware of love, they cannot be aware of hate, since it would be completely nonsensical to have two contradictory feelings against the same person at the same time.[293]

Nonsensical, i.e. "immoral."

The truth is that we meet on the level of the pairs of opposites, *inseparable* pairs of opposites, and there love and hate are two sides of the same coin. Anyone who admits to having unfiltered perception, which is rather unlikely since conventional "thinking" forbids it, will observe the following: The closer you are to a person or phenomenon the more love **and** hate.[294]

Friedrich Nietzsche left behind probably the pithiest words in the history of Western thought – apart from those of Jesus of Nazareth, with whom he sometimes competed:[295]

---

[293] Fromm, Erich (D.T. Suzuki, R. de Martino); *Zen Buddhismus und Psychoanalyse*, Frankf../M., 1981, p.131.

[294] "In order to see a thing completely, man must have two eyes, one of love and one of hate," Nietzsche, Friedrich; *Weisheit für Übermorgen*, München, 1994, p.74.

[295] In other places he tried to understand him. If he had known the Jesus literature, which was only unearthed after 1945 from Nag Hammadi, Nietzsche would perhaps be considered one of the better Jesus interpreters today.

My destiny is that I have to look more deeply, more cou-
rageously, more righteously into the questions than anyone ever before. Revaluation of all values, that is my
formula for an act of the highest order self-reflection of
mankind, which has become flesh and genius in me. But
my truth is terrible, because until now lies have been
called truth. One day my name will be the memory of
something monstrous, of a crisis like no other on earth, of
a decision, conjured up against everything what had been
believed, demanded and sanctified until then. I have the
greatest scope of soul that a human being has ever had. I
am not a human being, I am dynamite.[296]

Nietzsche asked even before Freud:

What you have to love, why do you always have to hate it
at the same time?[297]

I dare to take the (necessarily stuck in perspective) approach of an "answer": As a human being I only ever em-
body one of the two sides of the pair of opposites, which is
one of few that already has a generic term, namely Person.
My gender identity is based on the fact that I do not belong
to the other half. And then I experience myself as an incom-
plete half and am drawn to my opposite sex with irresistible
force. That which has such a power over me and is the very
epitome of my own incompleteness, that I must hate. Hate
is just as original as its counterpart, (falsely) called love.

The real question in all dualities, which we want to discuss here by the example of the psychologically most superficial pair of opposites, is: What is the essence of an *insepa-*

---

[296] Nietzsche, Friedrich; *Weisheit für Übermorgen*, München,1994,
p.310 (fragment) and Radio BR ?: Albert von Schirnding (supplement).

[297] Gamm, H-J.; *Standhalten im Dasein, Nietzsches Botschaft f.d.
Gegenw.*, München 1993, p.13.

rable pair of opposites? What is the commonality on both sides? What is the essence (commonality) of the *inseparable pair of opposites* love/hate? You could call it "relatedness as such." Hate always expresses oppressive relatedness, even if it pretends not to.

"True love," if it existed, would have to be found above the dualism level of love/hate, because the alleged love on the dualism level is only the reverse side of hate. The true love would then not be the love from the pair of opposites, which is only the positive side of hate, but "above" love/hate.

True love is on a different level than that of dualities.

> In order to see a thing completely, man must have two eyes, one of love and one of hate.[298]

Nietzsche suspected it! But he couldn't think it through at the time. If he had known the doctrine of dualities or had studied the two truths of Buddhism he would have gone far enough to see: Man has two eyes, one of love and one of hate, the latter is difficult for him to admit clearly. But in order to see a thing really completely, he needs to establish a supra-opposite third eye above the level of the pairs of opposites. This eye would be that of true love. The real problem with true love is:

> True love is properly understood only by the mental type, which is spiritually oriented.[299]

---

[298] Nietzsche, Friedrich; *Weisheit für Übermorgen*, München, 1994, p.74.

[299] Bailey, Alice; *Eine Abhandlung über sieben Strahlen* Bd. 5, Bietigheim, 1984, p.549.

Today it no longer makes sense to say: Thou shalt love! Morality has always been a false one because it has put the emphasis on one side of an inseparable whole and did not recognize that it is about transcending the level of dualities. Emphasizing one side of an inseparable whole makes no sense. Morality has never worked. Continuing to use the word will fail. A more realistic expression could perhaps be "ethos".

5.1.2 New question

Compared to other questions raised in books on Chinese Buddhism, every now and then a little is raised on this question:

> The unconditional, nondiscriminative Love and Compassion arising spontaneously from a direct experience of Sunyata, once one overcomes the attachment to Sunyata, is really a miracle of mankind which makes Buddhism the most unique and profound practical teaching.[300]

A direct experience of Sunyata, if it is not an "attachment" experience,[301] evokes spontaneous love of the unconditioned, non-differentiating kind, i.e. non-dual (true) love. Strong stuff. The fact that this is so rarely thrown in could be viewed favorably as an honest indication that writing about the concepts of Sunyata and the experience of Sunyata are two different things. The first question to be

---

[300] Wu, John C. H. & others; *Chinese philosophy, Vol. 2, Buddhism; Chinese Culture Series 1-6*; China Academy, 1972, p.265.

[301] Attachment is the opposite of detachment, that is, clinging, biting. To be attached to Sunyata is to think of Sunyata as *anything (except love-wisdom)*.

asked is whether a person is worthy of love – absolution. About man, Nietzsche said:

> But Zarathustra saw the people and was amazed. Then he spoke thus:
>
> Man is a rope, tied together between animal and superhuman – a rope over an abyss. A dangerous crossing, a dangerous going up, a dangerous looking back, a dangerous shuddering and standing still. What is great about man is that he is a bridge and not an end: what can be loved about man is that he is a transition and a downfall.[302]

Man can be loved. The downfall of the animal in him and the transition to the superman is worthy of love. Ken Wilber speaks of the halfway point of evolution. What happens in the halfway period? The first half is over, but the second has not yet begun. Now the psychological skills of the trainer are needed.

Thus, the study of Chinese Buddhism has revealed that it – like its colleagues from religion and philosophy – is constantly missing the mark in terms of bringing us what we need.

It is empty, without content, and yet it is Love. Or more precisely, it is the framework for Love. The opening to Love. The essential question of Buddhism would have been: Who can explain that Emptiness is Love? But the day is not yet done. Who has learned that *Emptiness is Love*?[303]

---

[302] Nietzsche in: von der Osten, Henning; *Über die Welt und über Gott*, Bielefeld, 1993, p.293.

[303] There is even a word for the **"indivisibility of Sunyata and karuna (compassion)."** The Sanskrit man is the most advanced, he has a word Sunyatakarunabhinnam, which means **EmptinessLoveInseparable**. This is the word to be explained. (Odin, op.cit., p.143).

The essential question, for future thinking, remains unanswered: What is Love? What kind of thinking makes Love available? What mental pathways enable an experience of Love? Which interpretation of the world allows Love? The greatest challenge of Buddhist tradition to evoke Love is: The direct experience of Sunyata (the "quasi-nothing"). The greatest challenge of the Western tradition says: "God is Love." What mental approach stimulates each one? What mental approach stimulates an experience that the "quasi-nothing" is Love, and what approach stimulates any experience that **God is Love**?

Claudia Schmölders has just published a book in the West called *The invention of love, famous testimonies from three millennia*. A good compilation and, yet, it would have been even better called: "Love awaits its invention." Can we explore the approach of what Love means for Dao, the Event, God or Emptiness, precisely within the whole "in which we live, and move and have our being?"

God, Dao, Event, Kong (Li) or Logos, the strongest words that we have produced, the words with the greatest "meaning," the words that point to something of which our friend Hegel said that you can't think of the Spirit big enough. They all want to say *Love*?

Anyone who loves knows that love cannot be said. Are these words (God, Dao, Event, Kong, Li or Logos) the concealments of love? Anyone who loves knows that love cannot be said, but it must be said. Are these words attempts on love?

In anticipation, we must immediately christen hypothetical love as *non-dual Love* because that love, which brings hate as an accompanying shadow, lies precisely on the level of dualities. It would have to be a Love which has no opposites. The dualities are mutually dependent. On the level of dualities, love conditions hate and hate conditions

205

love. The Love we have to explore is the Love that is not conditional – the unconditional Love.

So we ask, what is Love?

Since Bachofen's publications we know about the matriarchy of past times. Direct intuition (which usually comes only after a long, in-depth study of the topic) also knows that the slowly disappearing patriarchy only lasted a very short period in human history.[304] The difference of the sexes lies in this: men love to create sayings. This, in its highest sublimation, has produced religion and philosophy. If a man at the level of contemporary thought recognized the hollowness of all conceivable sayings, but wanted to create one more saying – a saying that says nothing, but says everything that can be said, and also the unspeakable – he would say:

> The polar paradox of everything/nothing is neither "everything/nothing" nor not "everything/nothing", but "~~everything/nothing~~".

This statement is, as you will see, the best – the **only** one. The realization of the true understanding of this saying transcends everything.[305]

If the expression "paradox" is understood as "self-cancellation," the "is neither nor is it not" is unnecessary to say. Then only: "The polar paradox of everything/nothing." If it was said that all things exist as polar paradox pairs, but only one among them is *the* pair par excellence – namely Mr. Nothing and Mrs. Everything – then it is enough to say:

---

[304] Again, Gebser is the only one I know who gives a name to the coming epoch: neither patriarchy nor matriarchy, but integrate.

[305] Which does not mean that anything changes.

"*The* polar paradox." If we want to say it even shorter, we say: "Polar Paradox," *abbreviated*: P.P.[306]

空空

Even simpler than Kong Kong is PP. Letters or characters are a quite recent invention in the evolution of the upright animal, in which the spiritual spark was implanted. Since now this composite being of animal body and spiritual spark can write, it is obsessed with wanting to make a "definitive" statement. The author of these lines is also shaken by this legacy. "I want the truth," is how the animal understood the spiritual spark. "I want something final." That is why the descendants of Mr. Nothing and Mrs. Everything sometimes say the 'final" wedding vows, *I do*. Unfortunately, it does not work. This final word has turned out to be divorceable (divisible). This final word also been refuted. To have to live without finality – the hopeless rebellion against it – is the "love of wisdom."

It means constantly becoming pregnant with new questions. Perhaps the essence of philosophy is just the question. So this paragraph ends with a question without which the question about love can never be asked. Indeed, the question quoted below and the question about Love is deeply and inextricably linked. Heidegger, once again, builds on

---

[306] "The best statement is one that does not fall into the net of words": it is "neither Being/Nothing nor not Being/Nothing," *it could be said to be the only statement*, following a stylistic device of Heidegger with an essential correction. ~~Being/Nothing~~. Heidegger himself did write: "Like ~~Being~~, Nothing would have to be written and thought of" (*Zur Seinsfrage*, Frankf./M., 1977, p.31), but he did not take this step because he did not know the Yuanqi equation as such.

his discovery that Western philosophy never figured out the essential:

> The essential origin of the being of that which exists is inconceivable. That which is actually to be thought is withheld. It has *not yet* become worthy of thought for us. That is why our thinking has not yet found its own way. We don't actually think yet. That's why we ask: what does thinking mean?[307]

5.2 Towards a hierarchy of disciplines

> The fact that the sciences are no longer understood as a unity is not due to the fact that they have become complex. The university has unfortunately divided knowledge into specialized disciplines; and each is forced into its ritual and vocabulary, which would not be necessary at all. Reject the fragmentation of knowledge, think of everything, don't let yourself be overwhelmed by the flood of information, resist the disenchantment of occidental thought and historical pessimism, because you are lucky to live at the end of this 20th century. Do not be dumbed down by anything, neither by fashions, nor by intellectual terrorism, nor by money, nor by power. Learn to distinguish the true from the false always and everywhere![308]

In her 1932 book with the epoch-defining and epoch-anticipating title "From Intellect to Intuition," Alice Bailey quotes a man named Ludwig Fischer:

> One way of advancing only is possible. The way is led by the intuition of minds of a more than average instinctive

---

[307] Heidegger, Martin; *Vorträge und Aufsätze*, Pfullingen, 1990, p.137.

[308] Sorman, Guy; *Denker unserer Zeit*, München, 1989, p.332.

sensitiveness; analytical reason follows, consolidating the position and making practicable the road for the rest of mankind. The advance into the unknown begins with a hypothesis, and a hypothesis is nothing but a more or less non-rational structure, obtained intuitively. Once it has been set up, it is compared in all its implications with experience, so that, if possible, the hypothesis can be tested and explained rationally.[309]

In the fifth week of 1997 alone, two programs by the Bavarian Broadcasting Corporation focused on interdisciplinarity. If the phrase by the cyberneticist Frederic Vester that "Reality is always interdisciplinary" applies to the fields of environmental technology and the natural sciences, how much more so with the humanities. A physicist from the University of Vienna said, "Interdisciplinarity is required everywhere, but not promoted."

On the first day of the sixth week of the year 1997, a man from the University of Potsdam repeated on Deutschlandradio Berlin, which had already been alluded to in other broadcasts, the proposed reformulation of Humanities into "Cultural Sciences." But as what has become so very clear in my work, the great problem lies in the term "science" – the interpretation by natural science with what it calls exactness. Science today means natural science. I might point out that this is a hopeless fight that cannot be won. The real classification, as it had existed for a long time, was either science and religion or science and philosophy or sometimes science and art. In my opinion it has to be called science and art. Why? Human use of language goes without saying (without ever having checked this) as a representation of reality. But it is not the case that we represent reality, but that we create reality with language. When-

---

[309] Bailey, Alice; *vom Intellekt zur Intuition*, Genf, 1986, p.109.

ever we speak, we are already creators! Whenever we speak we are making art more or less qualitatively, as the case may be.

If such a distinction applies to every human expression, i.e. for all disciplines of the humanities (which come from philosophy), then it is confirmed that philosophy is still what used to be called the "queen of sciences." We have to, and must want to, give up the "science" spoon. So, Philosophy is the Queen of the Arts:

> The areas of life are many. Special sciences develop for each of them. But life itself is a unity, and the more the sciences strive to deepen into individual areas, the more they move away from the view of the living world as a whole. There must be a knowledge that looks for the elements in the individual sciences to lead people back to full life. [...] The individual sciences are preliminary stages of the science aimed at here. A similar relationship prevails in the arts. The composer works on the basis of the theory of composition. The latter is a sum of knowledge, the possession of which is a necessary precondition of composing. When composing, the laws of compositional theory serve life, real reality. Philosophy is an *art* in exactly the same sense. All real philosophers were *conceptual artists*. Ideas, for them, became the materials of art and the scientific method became the artistic technique. Abstract thinking thereby gains concrete, individual life. The ideas become life forces.[310]

What is the nature of the form of art which is philosophy? Anyone knows the detailed psychological subtleties of, for example, Friedrich Nietzsche[311] and Jean-Paul Sartre,

---

[310] Steiner, Rudolf; *Philosophie der Freiheit*, Dornach, 1992, p.270.

[311] Nietzsche himself referred to himself in weighty places as a psychologist.

or of the ability of the late Heidegger to clothe essences of feeling in overwhelming beauty, or the Buddhists, will agree with me that these individuals were primarily psychologists. Philosophy is the highest of the arts, because it is actually psychology proper. This is because all other questions are derived from two questions: *What is being* and *who is man*. The current "scientific" psychology doesn't answer the first question at all and the second completely inadequately. It is about the real psychology of knowledge, which most likely could be referred to as spiritual psychology or esoteric psychology.

Philosophy, as psychology, is the highest of the arts. On a worldly level, this is a most profound, compressed, content-dense and loaded sentence of this work. Philosophy in its capacity as actual psychology is the queen of the arts. With philosophy, religion should also be mentioned here provided that it does not belong to rigid doctrinal "theology."

For Buddhism, the philosophical is rooted in the psychological.[312] Philosophy is applied psychology. I have always held Buddha to be one of the most decisive psychologists of humanity. Philosophy is still the better psychology – except perhaps for a few advanced Americans who are hardly recognized by anyone, or whose light is rarely correctly assessed by anyone.

When the most detailed psychology of the planet Terra (the Indian one) came to a land that, until then, was not interested in psychology (China), it hit the nail right on the head. The most important denominator of detailed psychology was highlighted: We are all (potentially) the Buddha.[313]

---

[312] Katz in: Tuck, Andrew P.; *Comparative Philosophy and the Philosophy of scholarship, on the western interpretation of Nagarjuna*, N.Y. 1990, p.92.

[313] Or currently?

211

Moreover, we can all experience this with the help of meditation and transcending the mind.

A thousand years later, the Americans imported this body of thought and – because of its ability to integrate – Western philosophy, for the first time in its history, gained a small lead over the continent from which it came.

5.2.1 The topos of Buddhism

Psychoanalysts very aptly call the babbling of a baby, or the sighs of relief from a big baby at his sexuality, deep music.

In a work of comparative religion, Holmes Rolsten draws a map from Augustine through al-Ghazali and Sankaracarya to Nagarjuna and puts on paper the following:

> In the Sunyata presence, intellect stops for mapless being there. The Music has no lyrics.[314]

This is music of the heights. This is the music that always plays. The best there is, the "peal of silence."[315] Beethoven described music as:

> ... a higher revelation than all wisdom and philosophy.[316]

One floor above Beethoven begins the sound of the Buddhas. I assert (from experience) a clear step model that

---

[314] Rolsten, Holmes; *Religious inquiry – participation and detachment*, N.Y., 1985, p.115.

[315] Heidegger, Martin; *Unterwegs zur Sprache*, Pfullingen, p.3.

[316] CD: Deutsche Grammophon: Beethoven; Symph.4&7.

is extremely informative to the question "what is (Chinese) Buddhism?"

Four levels:

1. the depth music of the baby

2. the stammering of the better philosophers (the more psychologically aware the better)

3. Boulez, Isabel Mundry, Frangiz Ali-zade, Lachenmann, Annette Schlünz, Tan Dun, Rihm, Chaya Czernowin, Ferneyhough, Eggert, Emmanuel Nunes, Dieter Ammann, etc[317]

4. the soaring music of the Buddhas[318]

For the first time, we are touching on the essence of Buddhism at the level on which it takes place. We said that the strongest approach to the question "What is the light?" is to repeat it. We go one step further and ask: Where does the light come from?

> "What is the awareness of the realm of Buddhas?" It is not something that can be known by consciousness (fei shih so neng shih).

非识所能识

---

[317] Some of the composers who stood out on my way for reasons not mentioned here.

[318] cf. Richard Wagner's Tristan: "Wie hör ich das Licht" ("How do I hear the light").

It cannot be known by consciousness. Consciousness falls within the category of discrimination. Were it discriminated, it would not be true awareness. True awareness is only seen in no-thought. Nor is it an object of the mind (I fei hsin ching cheih).

亦非心境界

It cannot be known by wisdom. That is to say, if one were to realize it by means of wisdom, then it would fall within the category of an object that is realized, but since true awareness is not an object, it cannot be realized by wisdom.

What Tsung-mi thus means by "awareness" is not a specific cognitive faculty but the underlying ground of consciousness that is always present in all sentient life. It is not a special state of mind or Spiritual insight but the noetic ground of both delusion and enlightenment, ignorance and wisdom, or, as he aptly terms it, the mind ground (hsin-ti).[319]

心底

Awareness can be considered a keyword. Zongmi (Tsung-mi, the 5th patriarch of the Huayan school) places awareness above wisdom. Awareness cannot be known, measured, imagined, conceived, deserved or achieved. Awareness is the hearing of the soaring music, the most powerful of all symphonies, the motionless sea of silence.

---

[319] Gregory, Peter N.; *Tsung-mi and the sinification of Buddhism*, New Jersey, 1990, p.218.

5.3 On rigor in the humanities

In order to be rigorous, the "humanities" must necessarily remain inexact. This is not a deficiency, but their advantage. In terms of performance, the implementation of rigor in the humanities always remains much more difficult than implementing the exactness of the "exact" sciences.[320]

It is not only difficult, it is almost impossible. How should the inevitable inaccuracy be evaluated? One could at most measure the degree of awareness of the inaccuracy. As said in the introduction, there are those who have nothing to say and know that they have nothing to say, and there are those who have nothing to say and do not know that they have nothing to say. The latter should then get the lower grades.

After all that has been said, it will be clear that it is impossible for a reader of my master's thesis to relive what I intended when I wrote it, because that would mean that he would experience the same associations, ecphorias, with every single word as I did. This can be excluded with complete certainty.

In any case, an evaluator would evaluate what he experienced while reading my work. What he experienced while reading my work and the work itself will always remain two different things. Even I, myself, do not read this work the same way twice. Roughly speaking, sometimes I read more its strengths, sometimes more its weaknesses, even in the same sentences. And the work as such does not exist. The work, *in itself*, really does not exist.

---

[320] Heidegger, Martin; *Gesamtausgabe, 3. Abteilung: Unveröffentlichte Abhandlungen, Band 65: Beiträge zur Philosophie* (Vom Ereignis), p.150.

亦非心境界 非識所能識

216

There is no objectivity, human or supernatural, that could capture this work "objectively." Ultimately, this work is made from the material, from which, according to the thought that bears the title Buddhism, all Things (Dharmas) are.

The dubiousness of grades is now very obvious. It would be more sensible for me to evaluate my own work, as I already wrote to one teacher from each of my two minor subjects – religious studies and philosophy. Now it's time for the major subject too. My own evaluation is: Sometimes I find it good, sometimes less. I find the strengths good, the weaknesses not. Could the work be without weaknesses? In view of the unalterable discrepancy of a real existing world of metaphysics – abstractions or ideas on the one hand, and a real existing language on the other hand – it is not possible to write a paper without weaknesses.

Of course, one could weigh the ratio of strengths to weaknesses, but such a weighing would be a simultaneous balancing of so many factors that to classify them into a system of six points seems to me, in any case, inappropriate here.

This work will go down in the history of non-alternative educational systems as the one that, with the help of the material it deals with (specifically, Faxiang Buddhism), clearly spells out that it is unassessable. The writer of this work is aware that he has reproduced the basic underpinning emphasized by Heidegger[321] but is a young thinker who has not yet published a statement saying **"Sometimes I think I can see that man is the medium of language, not vice versa."** At this point in the master thesis, which is called "An Appreciation of Chinese Bud-

---

[321] "Man behaves as if he were the creator and master of language, while it remains the mistress of man." Martin Heidegger in: Berendt, E.J.; *Das dritte Ohr*, Hamburg, 1990, p.117.

dhism," we are approaching a culmination. First it was said with Nietzsche, and above all with Wittgenstein and Buddhism, that a word has no meaning that can be fixed. Then, it was said that only through language is reality produced ('things are what the word makes of them by naming them'). To think these two basic realities together was already difficult. But only now comes the superordinate revelation about language, which is to be synthesized with the other two in just this superordinate relation: **The language speaks. Man does not speak, language speaks. The Word brings itself forth through (written) language. Man is the medium for the Word.**

Man speaks only by conforming to language.[322]

Whoever loves will give unconditional priority to a phenomenon and that is called education. The measure of value for philosophy is whether it has a psychological impact or not. Philosophy is education. The great philosophical teachers of the end of the century – Krishnamurti, Steiner, Sai Baba, Aurobindo – they all felt compelled to found schools. As long as every school is not a "Steiner, Montessori, Krishnamurti, etc. school," the individuals mentioned have not yet helped much. As long as children's school achievements experience their finality in an assessment, we will not know who we are. As long as artistic achievements experience their finality in an evaluation by a so-called critic, we will not know what art is for. And as long as art is distinguished between U+E (German abbreviation for the distinction between entertaining and serious), we will not know what art can mean today. Art is not there to be judged. Art gives individuals the opportunity to see what they want

---

[322] Heidegger, Martin; *Unterwegs zur Sprache*, Pfullingen, p.33. "Der Mensch spricht nur, indem er der Sprache entspricht."

and can gain from it. Verbalizations are art. An art critic or an evaluator of a master's thesis must be aware that his criticism, itself, is a work of art.

"Every man is an artist," was a message of respect for humanity portrayed as the basic character of an artist by art theorist and teacher of contemporary art, Joseph Beuys. The artist of the future will make the assessment of his work himself.[323]

Would it be so absurd, then, if the pupil himself also made the first criticism of his performance? The basic idea of Maria Montessori was that the progress in the development of a child (a learner, which would remain a learner throughout their whole life) should be measured only in comparison with oneself and not with others. The accuracy of this approach cannot be disputed. Who can judge how much effort is behind this master's thesis and who possesses the yardstick by which this effort could be uniquely measured? Of course, one can say that effort is one thing while the result of effort is another, and the latter should be evaluated. Apart from the fact that there is no objective result,[324] there remains a myriad of possible, completely different, criteria with which the "result" could be evaluated. Based upon some criteria in my own mind, this work performs worse but, on other criteria, it performs better. A discussion of possible criteria would be interesting. One of Krishnamurti's transformation-creating abilities was that he took words like achievement, discipline, concentration, learning, and especially attention into an entirely new realm

---

[323] Composer and Princeton University music professor Paul Lansky has already written a piece (Table's clear) that includes his son's commentary ("this is the most beautiful part"). The commentary is part of the piece (Radio Bayerischer Rundfunk 2, composer portrait by Uli Aumüller).

[324] I think that I have "proven" this with this work.

of being. He analyzes the root of the most avoidable fears of people as the mechanism of comparison. The German biographer of Krishnamurti and lecturer at the LMU Munich writes:

> Comparing or measuring oneself against something forms the foundation of our education system. This is expressed in exams and grades. Krishnamurti believes that all of our moral and religious structures are based on the principle of measuring or comparing.[325]

Krishnamurti exposes this principle as fundamentally *wrong* and as a major root of the world's ills. If the foundation is wrong then what, accordingly, happens in the first, second or third floor? One of the greatest assets of this master thesis is the rejection of a classification into the numbers one to six.[326] If this appears too "revolutionary," I would like to point out that I am not what in unphilosophical language is called "human," but am one who is establishing the negation of the Four-sentence proposition[327] of Sunyata as the **supra-opposite, causeless love and compassion**.

And it is impossible to let fourteen years of the state school system pass without comment, especially because I know in the deepest layer that schools not only fail to bring out human potential but, to some extent, undermine it – and, the hard truth, even mutilate it. One living philosopher (Peter Sloterdijk) called public education "the spectacle of mediocrity." My analysis is not as charitable.

---

[325] Gunturu, Vanamali; *Krishnamurti, Leben und Werk*, München, 1997, p.94.

[326] It goes without saying that I will "officially" accept a grade.

[327] As said, without having heard of the existence of Nagarjuna, Jizang, and Zhiyi before.

Since I am a total objector to gossip, I always direct criticism to the place it most affects. Since this could be my last direct encounter with state education, this must be stated here. Who is the state? The state is all of us. The first association with the word state is Plato. Philosophy, in any case, boils down to political philosophy as well. This is the basic approach of both Greek and Chinese philosophy.

Due to certain practical psychological themes, and above all because Sanskrit is what I consider to be a language invented for philosophical-Spiritual realities and I consider India to be the most viable of the three birthplaces of knowledge,[328] it is ultimately all about politics. What good is love if it does not become a political force?

Almost every text I read in my philosophy-oriented Sinology studies, and with hardly any change, began with the introductory sentence:

> The saints and sages of antiquity who sought to make the world work…

A certain amount of reassurance is realistic. After all, we live on a planet with a tradition in setting the right goals.[329] I introduced this work with a bang of pedagogy and it will soon end according to plan after a further pedagogical thunderclap that is intended to be understood politically. What we need are the techniques of intelligent love.

---

[328] Of the knowledge of the expiring mental age (Gebser's terminology): India, China and Greece.

[329] Even if this tradition has failed so far and, unfortunately, there is also a tradition in the wrong direction.

It could be that someone would come to understand the meaning of the expression 'to *mean* seriously what one says' by pointing to the heart.[330]

Peter Sloterdijk recently promised to examine the question of why the (left-wing) intellectuals of the 20th century have failed. I am eagerly awaiting the result. In reality, science/art is on the one hand while, opposite that, politics is on the other. This is the real relationship that must ultimately be taken into account. The failure lies on both sides. The survival of our species is still what is at stake.[331]

It all depends upon a complete reorganization of our political priorities. A minority of less than a quarter of the world's population is still consuming more than three quarters of all food and resources. The vast majority of humani-

---

[330] *Tractatus*, op.cit., p.457.

[331] In Sri Aurobindo's book "Das Abenteuer des Denkens" (Düsseldorf, 1986, S.106) the following word is found: "Love and power united could perhaps save the world in the end, but never love alone or power alone. That is why Christ must come again and that is why the followers of the religion of Mohammed, where it is not frozen, are waiting for a Mahdi."

Aurobindo omitted to mention that the Hindus are expecting Krishna again, the Jews are still waiting for the Messiah and in Buddhism the coming fifth Buddha, Maitreya, is expected and that (according to the esoteric tradition) it is one and the same person. In the forms of Chinese Buddhism the successor, Maitreya, announced by the historical Buddha, plays a particularly important role in Huayan.

In her book *Maitreya: I Come to Change All Things*, ethnologist Andrea Bistrich examines, among other things, the expectations of peoples: "The motif of the return of the bringer of salvation is alive in almost all cultures." (p.66) The collective memory of mankind seems to know about the present change of times (for the better). The quote at the beginning – "Much will depend on man's ability to renounce outworn structures" – is a Spiritual guideline of Maitreya. (From: Creme, Benjamin; *Messages from Maitreya, the Christ*, London, 1992, Message 74, 3.7.1979). [See also important additional note on page 249]

ty lives in poverty while the G7 countries (the greediest 7) continue to meet in order to celebrate and discuss their obscene misunderstanding of the world. On this course of blindness, irrationality and injustice will humanity perish – just as one person now perishes every two seconds from chronic malnutrition. The most important book for this class which refuses to recognize its unity with the world would be the Brandt Report. It clearly states in the title what is really at stake – *A Programme for Survival*: *The Report of the North-South Commission*, 1979.

At the inaugural Cancun Conference in (1981), the recommendations of this commission – which would have contributed significantly to solving the economic problems of both poor and rich countries – were pushed back by the Reagan and Thatcher dogmas. Third World delegations were left behind. At that time the world could have been set on the right course. Willy Brandt, himself, admits in the foreword to the Commission's theses that,

> …it remains true that during my time as Chancellor there were other priorities that occupied me and kept me from doing justice to the North-South issues. It is certainly the case that I did not pay sufficient attention to those colleagues who wanted to review and complement our priorities. (German version: p.13)

Who are the colleagues? Brandt names them:

> Quite a few writers, thinkers and scientists have given warning calls. (German version: p.27)

The fate of the writer, thinker, scientist and artist is that his existence makes little sense if he cannot force the politician to listen with an open mind. The master's thesis "On the Philosophy of East and West" has to end like this. Anything else would have been a waste of mental matter. The

223

essence of the sinologist had to be with a message on what The North-South divide is all about. More excerpts from Brandt's preface:

North-South relations are *the* great challenge of our time…. (German version: p.11)

I am convinced that it is short-sighted to say that the economic situation in the industrialized countries must first be addressed before more can be done for international economic cooperation. On the contrary, more cooperation with Third World countries would also benefit today's industrialized countries. (German version: p.10)

I underline: It is about the inclusion of all parts of the world. (German version: p.14)

History has taught us that wars cause hunger but we are less aware that mass poverty can, in turn, lead to war or end in chaos. Where there is hunger, there can be no peace. Anyone who wants to outlaw war must also ban mass poverty. In a moral sense, it makes no difference whether a person is killed in war or is condemned to starvation through the indifference of others.
   Never before has mankind had such a wide range of technical and financial resources at its disposal to deal with hunger and poverty. The enormous task can be mastered if the necessary common will is mobilized. (German version: p.23)

A historical process is not decided by resolutions or books, and privileged groups have rarely changed their attitude of their own free will. But arguments can play a role, and words can act like weapons. (German version: p.32)

Reducing the gap between "poor" and "rich" peoples, to reduce discrimination, to bring about step by step a chance for equality of life – all of his is not only in line with the pursuit of justice, which would be important enough on its own – corresponds to a healthy self-interest, not only for the poor and poorest countries, but also of those who are better off. (German version: p.24)

Our report is based on what is probably the simplest common interest: that humanity wants to survive – and, one might add, also has the moral obligation to survive. [...] Reduced to a simple common denominator, this report is about peace. (German version: p.19)

The North-South divide exists because of the manipulation and dominance of the world market by the richest nations. Therein lays the possible seeds of a final world war.

Peter Esterhazy writes: "It would be nice if there was a language in which one could say that 20,000 children starve to death every day, and say it in such a way that it sounds neither demagogic nor riotous, but that it means something and has consequences. Because at the moment it means nothing. Because at the moment it has no consequences."

Since 1981, 43 years have passed. That means 42 x 365 x 20,000 children have starved to death (approximately 314 million) due to an indisputable *world domestic politics (Weltinnenpolitik)* that completely ignores the situation, a term that Brandt already used in his 1979 report.

Together with my colleagues in the Commission, I am convinced that the peoples of this world not only must live together in peace, but can. The task is to free humanity from dependence and oppression as well as hunger and need. (German version: p.40)

Epilogue

Since the Frenchman reasoned "I think, therefore I am," there have been a number of modifications of this saying from the philosophical and humorous side. My correction reads:

> I realize what 'is' as the polar paradox, so 'I' 'am' neither everything/nothing nor not everything/nothing, but ~~everything/nothing~~.
>
> That,
> ~~everything/nothing~~
> and only that
> is the theory of all
> as an accurate, exact sign.
>
> **It is the God formula.**

The awareness of that[332] means, among other things, on the one hand the completion (fulfillment) of the phenomenon of longing and on the other hand the emptying of the possibility of forward-looking orientation.

> Krishnamurti calls this emptying death.[333]

---

[332] Which is only fully realizable for fractions of a second at the level we are at.

[333] Gunturu, Vanamali; *Krishnamurti, Leben und Werk*, München 1997, p.186.

226

Obituary

Aware of the **thought**[334] of the man whose seminar topics on the day of his death were announced as follows (of course, the seminars were not held anymore):

Spiritual overcoming of death in Daoism
(formerly Zhuangzi)

Physical overcoming of death in Daoism
(later Zhuangzi and Laozi)

The fact that for Wolfgang Bauer (Sinologist, 1930-1997) the physical overcoming of death was out of reach does not mean that it did not exist (and still could exist) and it also does not mean that he did not have a deep inkling about the Spiritual overcoming of death.

---

[334] Thinking and thanking are in our (German and English) language originally (etymologically) the same.

Closing words

> The strange thing is that in such a case I always want to say (although it is wrong): "I know that – as far as one can know such a thing." That is incorrect, but there is something right behind it.[335]

As I said, everything "philosophical" that could have been said would probably have been said differently, and my work is full of half-truths. Half-truths are half-truths because they are perspective, they cannot describe several or all perspectives. My work is, after all, at the beginning of the transition to the New Age and aperspectival philosophy (actually: eteology) will probably only emerge when thinkers from various "humanities" and special disciplines short-circuit each other.

But until, for example, the psychoanalyst, the connoisseur of the Indian Spirit, the strictly Christian theologian, the strictly Western philosopher, the neo-Marxist, the anthroposophist, the composer of New Music, plus the one who until recently was called the 'Orientalist',[336] the natural scientist and above all the thinking politician (if such a one is to be found.) will be capable of a common constructive language game,[337] we will probably muddle on as before for quite some time.

---

[335] Wittgenstein, Ludwig; *Über Gewissheit*, Frankf../M., 1994, p.246.

[336] All those mentioned are "special worlds" according to Husserl, who had a universal science in mind.

[337] That meets the challenge of the present to be transformative.

I hope to have contributed my part on the way to the aperspectival world for the time being. Having to use half-truths was pain enough for me. This work offers some useful and some indispensable conditions[338] for thinking about truth. Thinking about truth itself cannot be described, although it comes about for the most part with the help of words. Yet the words stand as synonyms of such refined conglomerations of abstraction and this in such a density and speed that cannot possibly be captured in conventional language. This density is rather the opposite of intensity, or the higher counterpart of intensity. Thinking about truth works, so to speak, with compact formlessnesses. Thinking about truth is therefore above the level of the concrete faculty of thought.[339] Thinking about truth takes place in a space which is in no way attached to the 'world' and remains aware of any mixture with the 'world'. Thinking about truth is to stay in the realm of intuition.[340] Thinking about truth is the response to impulses that come from a place that is infinitely far away and wants to pass on to us a realm of peace. Thinking about truth is the only thing we can call home without deluding ourselves. Thinking about truth flows from areas that completely address the suffering that this world has faced. In thinking about truth, the thinker experi-

---

[338] Of the preconditions are still some more, which found no entrance here, e.g. the acceptance of the natural law, which is called reincarnation, etc.

[339] This was what Heidegger meant when he wrote down his controversial words: "Science does not think." Two pages earlier in the same essay it says: "Even the fact that we spend years forcefully with the writings of the great thinkers does not yet guarantee that we think or are even willing to learn to think." (Heidegger, Martin; *Vorträge und Aufsätze*, Pfullingen, p.125). [See additional note on page 249]

[340] Albert Einstein: The intuitive mind is a sacred gift and the rational mind is a faithful servant.

229

ences that he does not exist as a person, but that he is the thinking of truth. Some quotes mention the previous limitations:

> I express, what I want to express, nevertheless always only with "half success." Yes, not even that, but perhaps only just a tenth.[341]

> There were thoughts before man had thoughts. Until now, he was not yet able to think the real ones because everything stumbled on the crutch of consciousness – he will rise above this crutch state.[342]

> The linguistic limits of our ability to express ourselves does not allow us to express more than one thought at a time before laying down in the statement a whole chord of different thoughts that are alive in our minds.[343]

But the incoherent thoughts, the dissonances, the "discordant notes," the unavoidable, only appear disharmonious from a limited perspective. The complement:

> Thinking must think against itself, which it is rarely able to do.[344]

Perhaps Arnold Schoenberg's statement about the "emancipation of dissonance" summed up, in a nutshell, the spiritual achievement of the 20th century.

---

[341] Wittgenstein, Ludwig; *Über Gewissheit*, Frankf../Main, 1994, p.475.

[342] Gebser, Jean; *Gesamtausgabe Band 7*, Schaffhausen, p.276.

[343] Gebser, Jean; *Gesamtausgabe Band 7*, Schaffhausen, p.266.

[344] Heidegger, Martin; *Aus der Erfahrung des Denkens*, Frankf../M., 1983, p.80.

"All speaking, by the way, is just silence in a cheeky manner. So let's talk. It's so cathartic to be able to speak when you know you're not going to say anything with it,"[345] says Mynona. "I wish for one EMPTY book, 100,000 pages strong." [346]

Pierre Boulez, the composer and conductor, is the founder of a 'band' called Ensemble InterContemporain. Some of the ever-changing members of this 'orchestra' have not yet awakened enough in their perception of the world to the extent that they could become completely at home in this New Music. To the sincerity of one of their musicians we owe the following words:

> Sometimes this music scares me, it acts as if we don't exist.[347]

A key quote from this master's thesis is "the philosophical, for Buddhism, is rooted in the psychological" continues:

> The belief in self, which Buddhism also holds to be a grammatical mistake, is deeply rooted in our desire that there be a self. Philosophical problems are a disease to be cured because life is a disease to be cured.[348]

---

[345] Must mean in the terminology of my work: nothing will be said with it.

[346] Cardorff, Peter; *Friedlaender (Mynona) zur Einführung*, Hamburg, 1988, p.84.

[347] TV: arte: Portrait Ensemble InterContemporain.

[348] Katz in: Tuck, Andrew P.; *Comparative Philosophy and the Philosophy of scholarship, on the western interpretation of Nagarjuna*, N.Y. 1990, p.92.

The belief in an "I" is a grammatical error, an error in the old way of notation. **The true state of entities is Emptiness.**[349]

Today we have music that is so "discontinuous" that it is impossible to sustain a constant which *shines through* in it. Even an "I" could only exist by drawing on some kind of continuity. At least it is confirmed in this one respect that what Beethoven called "a higher revelation than all wisdom and philosophy" can actually be contained in music. Freedom from the ego (freedom from the illusion of "I") as the characteristic of the integral structure of consciousness,[350] is equally the "goal"[351] of Buddhism and Krishnamurti – it is the healing of the disease we call life. This healing has already been made audible by the front line of our composers.

The first western philosopher to 'out' himself as God, which was what happened until then in his culture was reserved for religious mystics (apart from the churches), was logically named Mynona. Mynona is the reverse reading of Anonym(ous).

For God is neither this, nor that. God is *empty* ....

---

[349] Ng, Yu-Kwan; *T'ien T'ai Buddhism and early Madhyamika*, Hawaii, 1994, p.27.

[350] Gebser, Jean; *Gesamtausgabe Band 3*, Schaffhausen, 1978, p.677. "I-lessness is a deficient relapse into the magical, mere I-ness is a deficient persistence in the mental-rational. Only the overcoming of the I, which is an overcoming of both I-lessness and I-ness, places us in the I-freedom that the achronon and the diaphainon are able to preserve. I-freedom is freedom from the "I," is not I-loss or -renunciation, is not I-murder, but I-overcoming. I-consciousness was characteristic of the mental structure of consciousness. I-freedom is the characteristic of the integral structure of consciousness."

[351] "Goal" is in itself the wrong image, for there is nothing but the goal, and the goal is nothing.

Pedagogical supplements

(Excerpts from letters)

From a letter to a Religious Scientist (Michael von Brück):

Actually, I only wanted to write to you that I would be pleased if you would read my master's thesis before my oral minor examination with you, so that the encounter would be fruitful for both sides. Now the following has come about:

Shortly after finishing my master's thesis, my path of thought led me to Wilhelm Reich. The contextual draft of his book "The murder of Christ" – the whole book is more or less the insistent repetition of a contextual draft – meets with what I experience as the most urgent and essential resonance in me. Wilhelm Reich equates the inner Christ, among other things, with the life force and this in turn is the sexual energy whose subtlety Reich wanted to prove. The discovery of the "orgone energy" saw Reich's historical gift to mankind. I don't know if Reich knew the Indian Prana and the Chinese Chi (jap. Ki) concepts (I suspect not). In any case, there are some voices (among them one I trust) that accept the "orgone energy" as the natural scientific discovery of Prana, respectively Chi (Qi).

气

So I wanted to propose the "Murder of Christ" (newly translated with accompanying volume at Zweitausendeins) as my exam topic. In the course of time, because I need four topics for my sinological exams and at least two of them thematically refer directly to the "Murder of Christ" (these are on the one hand the Taoist sexology and on the other hand a book of an analysis of the Chinese national character called the "walled ego," another expression for what Wilhelm Reich calls 'character armor' or the armored man), something has crystallized which I would dare to share with you more easily if you had already read my master's thesis, which I sent to you.

One of my theses in my master's thesis is that, in a nutshell, religion and philosophy only really come into effect when they are recognized and realized as psychology – allow me for the moment to use the expression "High Psychology."

I am toying with the following idea: to demand that my work be taken at its word. Since there is no subject called "High Psychology," I would have to be given the opportunity to state what I mean – and this would make my three subjects one. So the thought of combining my three oral exams has come up. Doesn't it make sense for someone who has studied "humanities" to present his results at the end?

I can present these results only collected. It is simply one subject, it is the one subject of the (still hardly existing) true science of the human being.

The following 2 excerpts are from a book I had to read for the Religious Studies exam. This first excerpt from Hans-Jürgen Greschat's work:

In normal university life, learning and teaching is like school. Lecturers teach, students learn. Lecturers check students' learning outcomes. Lecturers direct learning, instruct students, praise the good and reprimand the bad. This forces students to reproduce, some do it verbatim, others guess what the lecturer wants them to say. In the end, students are frustrated and instructors have to work mightily to keep them motivated, which is what it's all about, it's the material that needs to be taught and learned. The opposite would be if students learned to produce instead of reproduce. Then everything would no longer revolve around the material, that is, around the results of previous research, but also around the research itself, not only around the "what?" but also around the "how?," not only around other people's skills, but also around one's own. Then lecturers would no longer have to motivate students, nor would they have to control and reprimand or praise them. Then the students themselves would take responsibility for their interest or lack of interest, because they could do what seems important to them, not to the lecturers, not to the material planners.

That sounds like a revolution. Its strategist is the American psychology professor Carl R. Rogers. His professional experience had shown him that people like to learn what interests them. Learning opens up new things to people who are interested, they expect something from learning and they get it if they persevere. Only when learning leads them into threatening situations do people resist new things. In an academic environment, many fear being embarrassed, humiliated, laughed at. When the threat disappears, so does the fear. Carl Rogers found out how much better people learn when they do something and when they set their own goals. The best learner is the one who is completely absorbed in something. It is also important that not someone else, but the learner himself perceives and evaluates his progress. If you learn in this way, you learn to learn. Why is this important? Because the sciences do not stand still, because the facts of today can only be the history of science in ten years. If you still want to be there, you have to keep learning.

If this is true, then it is important to be a learner, then it is unimportant to be a teacher. The lecturer becomes the *facilitator*. Because lecturers work longer in their field than students, they know more, they have greater experience and a wider horizon. This qualifies them as facilitators. They make their knowledge available. But they only pass it on to students who want it. They do not impose it on others.

Above all, this requires lecturers to trust their students. I trust them (and not only myself!) to solve problems. I do not require them to be interested in what interests me at the moment, to follow my ways. Everybody chooses the topic and the method that seems to be interesting and useful to them. I make myself available as a consultant and help them get material they want. I don't hide my view, but I express it as one among others, I don't impose it. In all of this, I learn a lot about myself. I learn to know and accept my limits. I learn which of my attitudes promote student learning and which hinders it.

Ever since I encountered the arguments of Carl Rogers and other humanistic psychologists (I wish it had been earlier in my life!), I have tried to apply them. Certainly, it is impossible to study religious science in this way alone. To do so, the university curriculum would have to be transformed. Moreover, there are students who want to be guided and examined. But at least one seminar per semester can be reserved for this. Within a general topic, everyone looks for his or her particular topic, which the students work on alone or in groups, in writing or as a presentation. The positive reaction of most of the participants encouraged me to continue after the first attempts. The results justified it. On their own responsibility, students have come up with original topics and convincing solutions. Religious studies should not lack imaginative researchers in the future.[352]

---

[352] Greschat; *Was ist Religionswissenschaft?,* Kohlhammer, 1988, p.134-38.

The second extract from Greschat:

The uninvolved observer:
Sometimes when we read or hear a thing, we don't give it a chance. Irritant words set off alarms in us, as if a bell were ringing. Then every bulkhead automatically closes, we are in a state of war, ready to defend ourselves, on diving station, encircled, loaded. And then we start firing, firing whatever is in our barrels, which is usually live ammunition. What threatens us, we want to shred or chase away. If it is stronger, we flee headlong, abruptly change the subject, quickly turn the page, or misunderstand as if nailed down.

The opposite would be if we remained open. Then there would be no alarm, no hastily fired judgments, no panic. Then, forgetting ourselves, we can invest all our energy in exploring that matter. First, of course, we must disarm, militarily speaking. And then we must strictly control our disarmament. For this we need the *uninvolved bystander, the impartial witness.*

Our defense mechanisms work automatically. Something triggers the alarm and everything else runs as if by itself. We react like robots, predictably, routinely, because we are programmed. There are many different programs about what, who and how we should or should not be. Some control our behavior since childhood, others we acquired later. If you identify one of our programs, we react robotically. What we identify with forces us, it takes away our freedom to react differently. It follows: If you want to be free, you have to give up your identifications! However, first the robot would have to recognize its programming. The uninvolved *spectator* helps it to do this. Our identifications are expressed in our evaluations and judgments. We can recognize what we identify with when we recognize *how* we evaluate, and this is what the uninvolved observer shows us.

It is a function of our consciousness. Occasionally he wakes up by himself, for example in moments of acute danger. After that, he continues to sleep. If you want to become aware, you have to awaken your consciousness and make an effort to keep it awake. To be aware means to be in the present. Walking while walking! Eating while eating! To be aware while perceiving! Daydreams, fantasies, past, future, all these are escape routes. Intellectualizing also acts on our consciousness as a sleeping pill. Intellectuals are characterized by the fact that they talk about something, but not that they experience something.

The uninvolved spectator resembles researchers who persistently and patiently observe something, an ant colony perhaps or a constellation. Whoever turns such observation from the outside world inward has the uninvolved spectator.

First you practice sustained awareness: while walking and so on. Then you practice watching: no longer being a walker while walking, but a witness who perceives the walking body. This witness perceives everything, no matter what you do. He perceives it, but remains uninvolved. He observes everything as it happens, without evaluating anything. He also does not give himself any grades for being a witness. If the person is afraid, his uninvolved witness registers: "Fear is there." He must not judge the fear: "it serves you right!" or "how terrible!" If the person does not fight against it anymore, fear, which in the automatic state triggers aggressive defense or panic flight, will pass as it came. This is because the uninvolved bystander turns off the involved ego. The I desires what it does not have, and what it has it fears to lose. As long as we are aware, we remain uninvolved: neither desire nor fear can spread within us. Then we have forgotten ourselves and are free to see truly objectively what is revealed to us.[353]

[353] Greschat; *Was ist Religionswissenschaft?*, Kohlhammer, 1988, p.134-38.

Here, an excerpt from AUROBINDO:

The first principle of teaching is that nothing can be taught. The teacher is not an instructor or supervisor, he is a helper and advisor. His task is to recommend, not to impose. He does not actually train the student's mind, but shows him how to perfect his tools of knowledge, helps him and encourages him in this process. He does not impose knowledge on him, rather he shows him how to gain knowledge for himself. The second principle is that the mental must be consulted in its own growth. The idea that the child must be pressed into the mold desired by the parents or the teacher is a barbaric insinuation untouched by knowledge. Rather, the child must be led to grow in accordance with its nature.... Everyone has in himself something divine, something proper, the possibility of perfection and power in whatever small measure God may offer it to him for acceptance or rejection. The task is to find it, develop it and use it. The main goal of education should be to help the maturing soul bring out the best in himself and perfect it for noble use.

The third principle of education is to go from the obvious to the remote, from what is to what should be. The basis of man's nature is almost always, apart from the past life of his soul, his environment, his nationality, his country, the soil from which he draws his food, the air he breathes, the sights, sounds, habits which are familiar to him.... The past is our foundation, the present our material, the future our goal and culmination. Each one needs his proper and natural place in a national educational system.[354]

---

[354] Aurobindo; *Vorbote eines neuen Zeitalters*, eine Einführung und Werkauswahl von Robert McDermott, Grafing, 1991, p.237-238.

A final letter to Hartmut Buchner who was my Heidegger teacher at LMU (University Munich) and author of *Heidegger und Japan* (Japan and Heidegger):

Dear Hartmut,

Now that I have taken off the academic straitjacket, I realize once again very clearly how heavy it weighed. In my master's thesis I wrote that it was impossible to let fourteen years of state education pass without comment, especially because I know in the deepest layer that schools not only fail to elicit human potential, but to some extent undermine and – the hard truth is, they even mutilate it. One living philosopher called public education 'the spectacle of mediocrity.' My analysis does not turn out to be so charitable. The quote about the spectacle of mediocrity is from Peter Sloterdijk. In a talk show, he then called a spade a spade: "When I look at my students, I ask myself, who killed their intelligence?" Sloterdijk is even more honest than I am. It is not mutilating, it is killing off what we call "education" and this is basically no different in the university than in school. Wilhelm Reich meant something similar in the book that brought him to my attention, "The murder of Christ." "Christ," for Reich, is the name of the true inner Self of every human being. Every baby is the Christ child. This is beyond our ken, as is the gradual murder of this true Self. Christ's murder happens all the time, that's why no one notices it. Our normal state is the murder of Christ. Reich attributed this – in his time – to the lovelessness towards infants and the killing of the suppressed libido. According to my conviction, where the murder of Christ (thus, permanently not knowing the Spiritual core of the human being) also rages through our misconception of education. Only, we do not know that we do not know.

Hans-Joachim Störig writes as a conclusion to his *Little World History of Philosophy* "...because leading 'professional' representatives of philosophy (think of

Heidegger and Wittgenstein) themselves undertake, demand or promise a 'destruction' and an end, a final completion of all earlier philosophies!...." *Here, for once, someone was fond enough of philosophy to take it seriously enough to acknowledge that it may already no longer exist.*

A key to this is what Heidegger says in his letter to you: He had "no evidence" that what he said "is consistent with reality" and, above all, "never binding as a statement."[355] Also Wittgenstein's most important contribution was to insist that a word *cannot* coincide with reality at all. It seems to me that to take this realization into account entails a way of being and being-in-the-world that is hardly ever accomplished, let alone the way of philosophy that it ultimately means. Unfortunately, I had to use the word "philosophy" here. There is no more philosophy. The age which began 500 years before Christ is now over. Its primal impulse has fizzled out under the keyword "self-overcoming of philosophy." If only at least this consensus of the last 'great' philosophers, (which is to condense a main concern of the *existence paradox*) would be finally taken seriously in my book, we would be actually at least the one step further!

Reich names the context in which the history of philosophy emerged thus:

> Culture and civilization have not been yet. They are just beginning **to enter the social scene**. **It is the beginning of the end of the** chronic Murder of Christ.[356]

Best regards,

Christian Reinhardt

---

[355] Heidegger, Martin; *Vorträge und Aufsätze*, Pfullingen, 1990, p.177-179.

[356] Reich, Wilhelm; *Christusmord*, Frankf. am Main, 1997, p.372.

Qi

Bibliography

Aurobindo; *Das Abenteuer des Denkens*, Düsseldorf, 1986.

Aurobindo; *Vorbote eines neuen Zeitalters*, Eine Einführung und Werkauswahl von Robert McDermott, Grafing, 1991.

Bailey, Alice; *Vom Intellekt zur Intuition*, Genf, 1986.

Ibid.: Abhandlung über die sieben Strahlen, Bd.5, Bietigheim, 1984.

Ibid.: Abhandlung über kosmisches Feuer, Bietigheim, 1987.

Bartley, W.W.; *Biography of Werner Erhard, the Transformation of a man*, N.Y., 1978.

Bauer, Wolfgang; *China und die Hoffnung auf Glück*, 1989.

Berendt, E.J.; *Das dritte Ohr*, Hamburg, 1990.

Bezzel, Chris; *Wittgenstein zur Einführung*, Hamburg, 1989.

Bistrich, Andrea; *Maitreya: "I come to change all things"*: Eine moderne Heilserwartung im interkulturellen Vergleich, München, 1996.

Brandt, Willy; *Brandt-Report, Das Überleben sichern: Bericht der Nord-Süd-Kommission*, Frankf./M, 1981.

Brück, Michael v.; *Einheit der Wirklichkeit*, 1986.

Buchner, Hartmut (ed.); *Japan und Heidegger*, Sigmaringen, 1989.

Butzenberger, Klaus; *Einige Aspekte zur Catuskoti unter besonderer Berücksichtigung Nagarjunas*, (unpublished paper).

Cardorff, Peter; *Friedlaender (Mynona), zur Einführung*, Hamburg, 1988.

Ch'en, Kenneth; *Buddhism in China, a historical survey*, Princeton, 1964.

Cheng, Hsueh-li; *Empty logic: Madhyamika Buddhism from Chinese Sources*, N.Y., 1984.

Cheng, Hsueh-li; *Nagarjuna's Twelve Gate Treatise*, Dordrecht, 1982.

Cleary, Thomas; *Entry into the Inconceivable, Introduction into Hua-Yen Buddhism*, Honululu, 1983.

Conze, Edward; *Eine kurze Geschichte des Buddhismus*, Frankf../Main, 1986.

Creme, Benjamin; *Maitreya, Christus und die Meister der Weisheit*; Göttingen, 1986.

Creme, Benjamin; *Messages from Maitreya, the Christ*, London, 1992.

Daiichi-Shobo (ed.); *T'ien-T'ai Buddhism: An outline of the fourfold teachings*, Hawaii, 1983.

Dethlefsen, Thorwald; *Gut und Böse*, München, 1989.

Ibid.: Oedipus, München, 1990.

Dümpelmann, *Leo and Hüntelmann*, Rafael; Sein und Struktur, Pfaffenweiler, 1992.

Ferber, Rafael; *Philosophie jetzt: "Plato,"* München, 1995.

Forke, Alfred; *Geschichte der neueren chinesischen Philosophie*, Hamburg, 1964.

Fromm, Erich (D.T. Suzuki, R. de Martino); *Zen Buddhismus und Psychoanalyse*, Frankf../M, 1981.

Fung, Yu-Lan; *A short history of Chinese Philosophy*, N.Y., 1967.

Gamm, H-J.; *Standhalten im Dasein*, Nietzsches Botschaft f.d. Gegenw., München, 1993.

Gebser, Jean; *Gesamtausgabe Bd. 3, Bd. 7*, Schaffhausen, 1978.

Ibid.: Verfall und Teilhabe, Salzburg, 1974.

Ibid.: Ausgewählte Texte, München, 1987.

Ibid.: Asien lächelt anders, Frankf../M, 1968.

Gregory, Peter N.; *Tsung-mi and the sinification of Buddhism*, New Jersey, 1990.

Ibid.: Traditions of Meditation in Chinese Buddhism,
Honolulu, 1986.

Greschat; *Was ist Religionswissenschaft?* Kohlhammer,
1988.

Gunturu, Vanamali; *Krishnamurti, Leben und Werk,*
München, 1997.

Han, T'ing-chieh; *San-lun hsüan-i chiao-shih,* Beijing,
1987.

Hecker, Hellmuth; *Asiatische Mystiker,* Wien, 1981.

Heidegger, Martin; *Aus der Erfahrung des Denkens,*
Frankf../M., 1983.

Ibid.: Parmenides, Frankf../M., 1992.

Ibid.: Vorträge und Aufsätze, Pfullingen, 1990.

Ibid.: Zur Sache des Denkens, Tübingen, 1969.

Ibid.: Gesamtausgabe Bd. 13, Frankf../M., 1978.

*Ibid.: Gesamtausgabe, Bd. 65: Beiträge zur
Philosophie (Vom Ereignis),* Frankf../M., 1989.

Ibid.: Holzwege, Frankf../M., 1994.

Ibid.: Zur Seinsfrage, Frankf../M., 1984.

Hempel, Hans-Peter; *Heidegger und Zen,* Frank./Main,
1992.

Henrich, D. (ed.); *All-Einheit, Wege eines Gedankens in Ost
und West,* Stuttgart, 1985.

Hirt, Josef; *Der Mensch und das Gesetz von Lust und
Unlust,* Institut Josef Hirt AG, Zürich, Switzerland,
1985.

Höffe, O. (Hrsg.); *Klassiker der Philosophie, Bd.2,*
München, 1995.

Huntington, C.W. jr.; *Emptiness of Emptiness, introduction
to early Indian Madyhamika,* Honolulu, 1987.

Ikeda, Daisaku; *Der chinesische Buddhismus,* München,
1987.

Izutsu, Toshihiko; *Philosophie des Zen-Buddhismus,* Hamburg, 1986.

Kempf-Bekkering, Friederike; *Der Kommentar Guo Xiangs zu den Kapiteln 1 und 2 des Buches Zhuang-zi*, (Magisterarbeit Sinologie).

Kennedy, Alex; *Buddhism for today*, Glasgow, 1988.

Keyserling Arnold; *Der Körper ist nicht das Grab der Seele ...*, Wald (Schweiz), 1982.

Krishnamurti, Jiddu; *Das Netz der Gedanken*, Hopferau, 1983.

Ibid.: Leben ohne Illusionen, Füssen, 1980.

Krishnamurti/Bohm; *The Ending of Time*, London, 1988.

Lexikon 2000, Bd.1, Stuttgart, 1970.

Lexikon des Buddhismus, Bern, 1993.

Liu, Ming-Wood; *Madhyamaka thought in China*, Leiden, 1994.

Madhyamika Dialectic and the philosophy of Nagarjuna, Institute of higher tibetan studies, Sarnath, 1985.

Maharaj, Sri Nisargadatta; *Ich bin*, Bielefeld, 1988.

Maturana/Varela; *Der Baum der Erkenntnis*, Bern, 1987.

Meltzer, Donald; Traumleben, *Überprüfung der psychoanalytischen Theorie und Technik*; München, 1988.

Modell, Arnold, H; in: *Psyche, Zeitschrift f. Psychoanalyse*, Stuttgart, März 1984.

Murti, T.R.V.; *Central Philosophy Of Buddhism, Study Of The Madhyamika System*, London, 1978.

Nagao, Gadjin; *Foundational standpoint of Madhyamika*, N.Y., 1990.

Nagao, Gadjin; *Madhyamika and Yogacara*, N.Y., 1991.

Needham, J.; *Science and Civilisation in China Bd.2*, London, 1956.

Newland, Guy; *The two truths in the Madhyamika of the Ge-luk-ba Order of Tibetan Buddhism*, N.Y., 1991.

Ng, Yu-Kwan; *T'ien T'ai Buddhism und early Madhyamika*, Hawaii, 1994.

Nietzsche, F.; *GesamtaufgabeBd.III/1: Geburt der Tragödie. Unzeitgemäße Betrachtungen*, Berlin, N.Y., 1984.

Novalis; *Aphorismen*, Frankf./M., 1992.

Odin, Steve; *Process Metaphysics and Hua-Yen Buddhism*, N.Y., 1982.

Pandeya, Ram Chandra; *Nagarjuna's philosophy of No-Identity*, Delhi, 1991.

Pannikar, Raimon; *Das Schweigen Gottes. Die Antwort des Buddha für unsere Zeit*, München, 1992.

Powell, James N.; *Das Tao der Symbole*, München, 1989.

Reich, Wilhelm; *Christusmord*, Frankf. am Main, Zweitausendeins, 1997.

Rhinehart, Luke; *"Das Buch EST,"* München, 1983.

Rolsten, Holmes; *Religious inquiry – participation and detachment*, N.Y., 1985.

Safranski, Rüdiger; *Ein Meister aus Deutschland, Heidegger und seine Zeit*; München Wien, 1994.

Sartre, Jean-Paul; *Das Sein und das Nichts*, Hamburg, 1995.

Schulte, Joachim; *Wittgenstein, eine Einführung*, Stuttgart, 1989.

Share International magazine, Amsterdam, September 1992, April 2000.

Shih, Heng-ching; *The Syncretism of Chan and Pure Land Buddhism*, N.Y., 1992.

Shinohara, Koichi + Schopen, Gregory (editors); *From Benares to Beijing, Essays on Buddhism and Chinese Religion*, Oakville, 1992.

Singh, Jaideva; *Introduction to Madhyamika Philosophy*, Motilal Banarsidass, 1987.

Sloterdijk/Macho; *Weltrevolution der Seele*, Zürich, 1993.

Smothermon, Ron M.D.; *Drehbuch für Meisterschaft im Leben*, Bielefeld, 1987.

Ibid.: Play Ball, The miracle of children, San Francisco, 1983.

Sorman, Guy; *Denker unserer Zeit*, München, 1989.

Steiner, Rudolf; *Philosophie der Freiheit*, Dornach, 1992.

Stingelin, Martin; *Nietzsches Lichtenberg-Rezeption*, Fink-Verlag, 1996.

Störig, Hans-Joachim; *Neuausgabe der "kleinen Weltgeschichte der Philosophie."*

Stolz, Fritz; *Grundzüge der Religionswissenschaft*, Göttingen, 1988.

Suzuki, D.T.; *Leben aus Zen*, Frankf../M., 1973.

Swanson, Paul L.; *Foundations of T'ien T'ai Philosophy*, Berkeley, 1989.

Tuck, Andrew P.; *Comparative Philosophy and the Philosophy of Scholarship*, N.Y. 1990.

Volkmann-Schluck, K.-H.; *Interpretationen zur Philosophie Nietzsches*, Frankf../M., 1968.

Waardenburg, Jacques; *Religionen und Religion*, Berlin, 1986.

Waardenburg, Jacques; *Perspektiven der Religionswissenschaft*, Würzburg, 1993.

Wehr, Gerhard; Jean Gebser, *Individuelle Transformation vor dem Horizont eines neuen Bewusstseins*, Petersberg, 1996.

Wilber, Ken; *Halbzeit der Evolution*, Frankf../Main, 1996.

Wittgenstein, Ludwig; *Über Gewissheit*, Frankf./M., 1994.
Ibid.: Tractatus logico-philosophicus, Frank./M., 1993.

Wright, Arthur; *Studies in Chinese Buddhism*, New Haven and London, 1990.

Wu, John C. H. & others; *Chinese Philosophy, Vol. 2, Buddhism; Chinese Culture Series 1-6*; China Academy, 1972.

Zhang, Qingxiong; *Xiong Shilis Neue Nur-Bewusstseins-Theorie*, Bern, 1993.

Additional Notes

Addition to footnote #101 on Page 68:

The exact Spiritual science consists of the precise terminology used in Alice Bailey's and Benjamin Creme's books. Here you can find the language which matches one-to-one with the multiple different levels of life and the constitution of Man. In these books you will also find that there are seven ways of thinking; so the structure for the criteriology (p.49 and p.99) is already given.

Addition to footnote #331 on Page 222:

According to Gebser: "Figures like Zarathustra, Confucius, Zhuangzi, Laozi, Buddha, Mahavira, Socrates, Platon, but above all like Jesus Christ do not appear by chance just in the moment when a mutation takes place. And without one therefore doing prognostics, let alone prophecy, it should be obvious that also this time, in the moment of the now taking place mutation, this mutation will experience an incarnation. That this incarnation, however, should be of a different kind and of a different nature this time, since it must manifest itself no longer *in time*, but in the time-free, namely that it will be of a transparent kind, this will emerge from the following...." (*Gesamtausgabe*, Band 3, Schaffhausen, 1978, p.399) (In the English version: *The Ever-Present Origin*, part 2, chapter 2, "The Climate of the New Mutation" p. 294-300).

Addition to footnote #339 on Page 229:

I would like to draw your attention to the *Gottesformel*, "The God formula" (622 pages), developed by Swiss author Thomas M. Waldmann. His book revolves around the same core ideas as mine, although he approaches the topic from the perspectives of mathematics and physics – which he studied. Thomas is looking for a publisher to translate his book into English: https://www.gottesformel.ch/